WHY THE IRAQI RESISTANCE TO THE COALITION INVASION WAS SO WEAK

STEPHEN T. HOSMER

Prepared for the United States Air Force

PROJECT AIR FORCE

The research described in this report was sponsored by the United States Air Force under Contracts F49642-01-C-0003 and FA7014-06-C-0001. Further information may be obtained from the Strategic Planning Division, Directorate of Plans, Hq USAF.

Library of Congress Cataloging-in-Publication Data

Hosmer, Stephen T.
    Why the Iraqi resistance to the coalition invasion was so weak / Stephen Hosmer.
    p. cm.
    Includes bibliographical references.
    ISBN 978-0-8330-4016-9 (pbk. : alk. paper)
    1. Iraq War, 2003– 2. Iraq—Armed Forces—Operational readiness. 3. Iraq—History—1991–2003. I. Title.

DS79.76.H68 2007
956.7044'3409567—dc22

2007014369

The RAND Corporation is a nonprofit research organization providing objective analysis and effective solutions that address the challenges facing the public and private sectors around the world. RAND's publications do not necessarily reflect the opinions of its research clients and sponsors.

RAND® is a registered trademark.

Published 2007 by the RAND Corporation
1776 Main Street, P.O. Box 2138, Santa Monica, CA 90407-2138
1200 South Hayes Street, Arlington, VA 22202-5050
4570 Fifth Avenue, Suite 600, Pittsburgh, PA 15213-2665
RAND URL: http://www.rand.org/
To order RAND documents or to obtain additional information, contact
Distribution Services: Telephone: (310) 451-7002
Fax: (310) 451-6915; Email: order@rand.org

Preface

Coalition forces in Operation Iraqi Freedom (OIF) were able to take down Saddam Hussein's regime in less than three weeks, at the cost of relatively few Coalition casualties. This monograph draws on information derived primarily from interviews with and interrogations of senior Iraqi military and civilian officials, to examine why the Iraqi resistance in March and April 2003 was so weak. The research focused on two questions: (1) Why did the Iraqi Regular Army and Republican Guard forces do so little fighting? and (2) Why did Iraqi leaders fail to adopt certain defensive measures that would have made the Coalition's task more difficult and costly?

These two questions encompass a number of related issues. The monograph examines the battlefield consequences of Saddam Hussein's strategic misjudgments and preoccupation with internal threats, the poorly designed and executed Iraqi military strategy and operations, the weak motivation and morale that permeated all ranks of the Iraqi military, and the superiority in combat capability enjoyed by the Coalition forces. It concludes with observations about why decisionmakers should be careful about the lessons they may seek to draw from OIF, how OIF paved the way for the insurgency that has followed in Iraq, and how OIF may influence the behavior of future United States adversaries.

The monograph is intended for the use of military and civilian officials concerned with the management, planning, and conduct of U.S. operations to deter and counter threats to U.S. interests from enemy regimes and other hostile actors.

The research for this monograph was sponsored by the Director, Plans and Programs, Headquarters, Air Combat Command, and was part of a larger study of OIF conducted within the Strategy and Doctrine Program of RAND Project AIR FORCE. The research findings also supported a larger study of OIF conducted within the Strategy, Doctrine, and Resources Program of RAND Arroyo Center. The Arroyo Center research was cosponsored by the Deputy Chief of Staff, G-3, and the Deputy Chief of Staff, G-8.

RAND Project AIR FORCE

RAND Project AIR FORCE (PAF), a division of the RAND Corporation, is the U.S. Air Force's federally funded research and development center for studies and analyses. PAF provides the Air Force with independent analyses of policy alternatives affecting the development, employment, combat readiness, and support of current and future aerospace forces. Research is conducted in four programs: Aerospace Force Development; Manpower, Personnel, and Training; Resource Management; and Strategy and Doctrine.

Additional information about PAF is available on our Web site at http://www.rand.org/paf.

RAND Arroyo Center

The RAND Arroyo Center is a federally funded research and development center sponsored by the United States Army.

Additional information about RAND Arroyo Center is available at http://www.rand.org/ard.

Contents

CHAPTER SIX
Superior Military Capabilities Gave Coalition Forces an Overwhelming Advantage

CHAPTER SEVEN
Concluding Observations

Summary

In Operation Iraqi Freedom (OIF), American forces were able to capture Baghdad and depose Saddam Hussein's regime within a period of less than three weeks, at the cost of relatively few U.S. killed and wounded. The British units that constituted the other part of the Coalition's invasion force captured Basra, Iraq's second-largest city, also with minimal casualties. Drawing upon information derived primarily from interviews with former senior Iraqi civilian and military officials, this monograph focuses on two questions relating to the rapidity and ease of that victory: (1) Why did the vast majority of Iraqi forces fail to offer significant or effective resistance? and (2) Why did the Iraqi leaders fail to adopt certain defensive measures that would have made the Coalition invasion more difficult and costly?

The analysis shows that the rapid collapse of Iraqi resistance was due to a combination of the following:

- Saddam's strategic miscalculations and preoccupation with internal threats
- the flawed Iraqi strategy, poorly managed and executed battlefield operations, and inferior equipment
- the poor motivation and morale of the Iraqi Regular Army and Republican Guard forces
- the superior firepower and other warfighting capabilities of U.S. forces.

Any one of these shortcomings might have compromised an effective Iraqi defense; collectively, they ensured a monumental rout.

Saddam Made Strategic Miscalculations

A key reason for the weak Iraqi defensive performance was Saddam Hussein's strategic miscalculations about the threat Iraq faced in early 2003. Saddam believed that (1) war with the United States could be avoided, (2) if war occurred, the United States would not invade Iraq, but would confine its operations to limited air attacks, and (3) in the unlikely event an invasion occurred, the Iraqi resistance would be sufficient to cause the United States and its Coalition allies to accept a negotiated political settlement that would leave his regime in power. (See pp. 18–27.)

Saddam's propensity for strategic miscalculation can be attributed to his congenital optimism, excessive self-confidence, and poor understanding of international and military affairs. The erroneous assumptions underlying his decisions went unchallenged because he was surrounded by sycophants and equally uninformed subordinates who were fearful of telling him truths that they believed he did not want to hear. The climate of fear Saddam engendered within Iraq nurtured a culture of lying, whereby senior military officers routinely misled Saddam about the readiness and fighting will of their forces. (See pp. 11–15.)

Because Saddam was the dominant decisionmaker in Iraq, his strategic misjudgments shaped Iraq's political and military behavior in the run-up to and conduct of the 2003 war. By disregarding the potential peril his regime faced after September 11, 2001 (9/11), Saddam failed to take the timely political steps—such as offering immediate and full cooperation to international arms inspectors—that might have helped to fend off a U.S. attack. The Iraqi leader's misperception of the threat fostered a lack of urgency in Iraqi defensive preparations, which often were ad hoc and last-minute. Saddam's confidence that the Iraqi military, using the strategy he had mandated, possessed the capability to force a political settlement with the Coalition, even in the event of an invasion, led him to eschew more draconian defensive options, such as the systematic use of scorched-earth and urban-warfare measures, that might have made OIF more difficult and costly for the Coalition. (See pp. 27–29.)

Saddam Was Preoccupied with Internal Threats

Saddam believed that much of the Iraqi military and populace would fight to defend Iraq; however, he trusted neither group as far as his own personal security and that of his regime were concerned. Saddam had been the target of multiple uprisings, coups, and assassination attempts; as a result, he gave priority to the preservation of his personal rule and his own security above all other matters. This overriding concern with internal security measures weakened Iraqi defenses against external attack. (See p. 31.)

To escape attacks on his person, Saddam moved frequently, conducted business from a variety of safe houses, refused to use the telephone, and limited information about his movements to a very small circle. To forestall coups, Saddam filled Iraq's key defense positions and battlefield commands with members of his family and his Tikriti clan, even though such persons often were, at best, only marginally competent in the military arts. He also established multiple competing military and militia organizations, with separate chains of command, in order to guard against anti-regime collusion; strictly controlled all troop and equipment movements in the country; and forbade the deployment of Regular Army or Republican Guard units inside Baghdad. To deter potential uprisings, Saddam positioned military units to prevent the infiltration of insurgent elements from Iran and ordered his security operatives and Ba'ath Party officials to keep close watch over the Iraqi civilian population. (See pp. 32–35.)

Saddam's preoccupation with internal defense made a successful decapitation air strike to remove him problematic. It also reduced the possibility that any "shock and awe" effects created by the simultaneous bombing of dozens of leadership and other key targets would cause Saddam's regime to "crumble." However, Saddam's focus on internal threats also undoubtedly weakened Iraqi capabilities to counter a conventional invasion: It forestalled the adoption of an effective defensive strategy, degraded the quality of Iraq's military leadership and battlefield decisionmaking, and prevented the coordination and unified command of the Iraqi forces charged with resisting the Coalition advance. (See pp. 36–39.)

Iraq's Military Strategy and Operations Were Poorly Designed and Executed

The warfighting strategy that Saddam imposed on his forces did little to effectively support his overarching political-military objectives of protracting the conflict, maximizing U.S. casualties, and thereby creating pressures for a negotiated solution that would leave his regime in place. Indeed, the defensive scheme he adopted hastened Iraq's defeat by failing to exploit potential options for prolonging the conflict and maximizing Coalition casualties. (See pp. 41–42.)

Among other shortcomings, Saddam's defensive scheme left most of the Iraqi Regular Army divisions in southern Iraq oriented to counter a threat from Iran and not well-positioned to meet an invasion from Kuwait. These units, along with most of the Regular Army divisions situated along the Green Line facing Kurdish-controlled territory in northern Iraq, remained close to their prewar deployment areas throughout the conflict. His decision to have Republican Guard and Regular Army divisions defend Baghdad from distant external defensive locations made those divisions extremely vulnerable to piecemeal destruction by U.S. air and ground forces. The immediate defense of the cities was left largely to politically reliable, lightly armed militias, and to Special Republican Guard units in the case of Baghdad. However, no fixed defenses or barricades were erected in the cities that could have provided strong fighting positions for these forces. Measures that could have slowed the U.S. advance toward Baghdad, such as the systematic mining of roads, destruction of bridges, and flooding of choke points, were not incorporated in the Iraqi defensive scheme. (See pp. 42–55.)

Moreover, Iraqi defensive operations were poorly managed and executed. These failures resulted from the Iraqi forces' inept military leadership, dysfunctional command arrangements and practices, poor situational awareness, counterproductive positioning on the battlefield, and poor training—even in skills as basic as marksmanship. The most egregious example of Saddam's wrongheaded battlefield management was his April 2nd order to move Iraqi divisions defending against the U.S. forces advancing from the south of Baghdad (which Saddam labeled a "strategic deception"), to the north of the capital in order to meet the "real" attack, which he suddenly concluded would be coming from Jordan. (See pp. 55–74.)

Aside from such mismanagement, Iraqi forces were further disadvantaged throughout the conflict by the fact that much of their armor and other military equipment was old and markedly inferior to that of the Coalition. (See pp. 74–76.)

Poor Motivation and Morale Decisively Undermined the Iraqi Defense

The central reason for the lack of Iraqi resistance in OIF was the Iraqi military's extremely poor motivation and morale. Events showed that the vast majority of the officers and troops in the Regular Army, Republican Guard, and Special Republican Guard did little if any fighting, and that they mostly deserted their units before being engaged by Coalition ground forces. In the course of the march up to Baghdad, U.S. ground forces rarely confronted cohesive enemy units of even battalion size. When major combat ended, not a single organized Iraqi military unit remained intact, because all the Iraqi troops that had survived the war had "self-demobilized" by going home. (See p. 77.)

This lack of fighting will and the high desertion rate were attributable to (1) the harsh service conditions that had depressed morale in Iraqi ranks even before the outbreak of hostilities, (2) the widespread conviction on the part of Iraqi officers and enlisted personnel that resistance against technologically superior U.S. forces would be futile, and (3) the fact that Iraqis of high and low rank saw little, if any, reason to fight and die for Saddam and his regime. The limited resistance that Coalition forces encountered mainly came from Saddam Fedayeen and Ba'athist militiamen, who had a major stake in the regime's survival, and from foreign jihadists, who were committed to defending a Muslim state against foreign infidels. (See pp. 77–86, 98–104.)

Desertions became commonplace, because the threat of eventual punishment that had previously deterred would-be deserters from fleeing their units was no longer credible once it appeared that Saddam would be overthrown. Senior Iraqi officers no longer attempted to enforce discipline in their units, and they frequently sanctioned and facilitated the desertion of their troops. (See pp. 86–90.)

The physical and psychological effects of U.S. air attacks also had a major influence on Iraqi battlefield behavior. The lack of any Iraqi air defense, combined with the precision and lethality of U.S. air strikes, proved devastating to both Iraqi military equipment and troop morale. The prospect of air attacks motivated Iraqi soldiers to stay away from their armored vehicles and artillery, and engendered fears among the troops about their personal survival and the safety of their families. Former Iraqi commanders testified that U.S. bombing prompted massive numbers of their troops to abandon their equipment on the battlefield, desert, and return home. (See pp. 90–97.)

The effects of Coalition psychological operations (PSYOPS) on Iraqi morale and behavior are more difficult to gauge. The surrender of Iraqi troops was a principal PSYOPS objective. That comparatively few Iraqis surrendered suggests that PSYOPS effects were limited. However, Iraqi troop behavior did conform to the PSYOPS appeals for desertion and weapon abandonment. The entry of U.S. forces into Baghdad was a major psychological shock to Iraqi military and civilian leaders in the capital, and it quickly undermined any remaining will to resist. When Saddam abandoned Baghdad on April 10, there were no longer any forces in the city for him to command. (See pp. 104–112.)

Superior Military Capabilities Gave Coalition Forces an Overwhelming Advantage

The Coalition's domination of the battlefield in OIF was also due to its capability to deploy well-equipped and highly trained and motivated fighting forces. The Coalition's objective of securing a prompt, low-casualty takedown of Saddam's regime was also facilitated by a battle plan that identified Baghdad as the Iraqi regime's center of gravity and provided for a scheme of maneuver that would allow U.S. forces to seize the capital rapidly. (See p. 113.)

In virtually every aspect of the fighting, Coalition forces demonstrated a marked superiority over their Iraqi opponents. The discrepancy in capabilities was particularly telling in the virtual immunity of Coalition armor to enemy fire, the ability of Coalition ground and air forces to deliver accurate, lethal fire on Iraqi targets and to attack those targets at standoff ranges and at night. The Coalition's ability to maneuver ground forces rapidly and sustain them over long distances also undermined the Iraqi ability to mount a coherent defense. (See pp. 113–121.)

Be Careful About Drawing Lessons from OIF

Military and civilian decisionmakers should be careful not to draw unwarranted lessons from OIF, particularly the notion that high-tech weaponry and communications will inevitably enable smaller-sized U.S. ground forces to be decisive against larger-sized, but less high-tech enemy forces in future conflicts. Decisionmakers should also be cautious about extrapolating operational lessons, such as whether invasions can be conducted at minimal cost in U.S. casualties in the absence of extended preparatory air campaigns. The extraordinary battlefield advantages that Coalition forces enjoyed in Iraq during March and April 2003 may not be replicated in future conflicts. (See pp. 124–125.)

The Iraqi military proved to be an extremely weak and inept foe in conventional conflict. While many of the Iraqi military shortcomings evident in OIF paralleled those observed 12 years earlier in Operation Desert Storm, the Iraqi military establishment that the Coalition faced in OIF was substantially more debilitated and hollow than was the enemy the United States and its allies faced in 1991. As a consequence, an Iraqi battlefield performance that was poor in 1991 was even worse in 2003. (See pp. 125–128.)

The Coalition benefited greatly both from what Saddam Hussein did and from what he did not do in the run-up to and conduct of OIF. The Iraqi leader's strategic misjudgments, propensity to focus on internal threats, poor defensive schemes and command appointments, and inept battlefield management significantly weakened the Iraqi military's capability to mount even a semblance of an effective defense. Indeed, it is difficult to think of other actions that Saddam might have taken, short of unconditional surrender, that would have proven more beneficial to the Coalition cause than the policies and practices that he actually adopted. (See p. 129.)

But what Saddam did not do was perhaps even more important. Had the Iraqi leader held a less benign view of the Coalition's intentions and recognized early on that his regime was in serious peril, he might have adopted scorched-earth tactics, urban-centered defenses, and other courses of action that could have increased the costs of OIF to both the Coalition and to the Iraqi people. (See pp. 129–130.)

OIF Paved the Way for the Insurgency That Followed

Despite speculation to the contrary, Saddam did not plan for a protracted guerrilla war after an Iraqi defeat in the conventional conflict. There were, however, a number of Iraqi actions before and during OIF that helped facilitate and shape the insurgency that has emerged in Iraq, including the large-scale arming of Ba'athist and other Saddam loyalists, the widespread dispersal of munitions and weapon stockpiles, the release of criminals from Iraqi prisons, the movement into Iraq of thousands of highly motivated foreign jihadists, the recruitment of Fedayeen Saddam militiamen and other persons willing to mount suicidal or near-suicidal attacks against U.S. forces, and the employment of unconventional tactics and weapons that eventually would become the hallmark of Iraqi insurgent operations. (See pp. 131–134.)

Importantly, the rise of insurgency in Iraq was also facilitated by the magnitude and nature of the Iraqi collapse, which was marked by the desertion of essentially the entire Iraqi military, security, and governmental structures. This massive flight from duty stations released into the Iraqi countryside numerous military officers and rank-and-file militia fighters, security and intelligence personnel, and Ba'athist officials who possessed the skills, resources, and potential motivation to mount and sustain a resistance against the occupation. (See pp. 133–134.)

The massive desertions also deprived the Coalition of the indigenous military forces and civilian officials that Coalition planners had counted on to help stabilize and secure Iraq. The small size of the OIF invasion force magnified the harmful effects resulting from the absence of any compensating indigenous assets. Indeed, without the active assistance of organized Iraqi military and police forces, Coalition troops lacked the numerical strength to promptly stabilize the country, which opened the way for widespread looting and lawlessness that made reconstruction more difficult and costly and undermined public support for the occupation. (See pp. 134–139.)

The lessons for future U.S. war planners seems clear: When taking down an enemy government or otherwise invading a foreign land, U.S. forces must be both appropriately configured and sufficiently robust to promptly establish firm control over the areas they occupy, to guard national borders, and to secure enemy arms depots and other sensitive sites. (See pp. 138–139.)

Even if the United States had sent larger forces to Iraq and had not disbanded the Iraqi military or banned full members of the Ba'ath Party from government employment, and, indeed, had taken other actions to dissuade potential opposition, such as holding early elections, some degree of armed resistance in Iraq was probably inevitable. However, a substantially larger U.S. military force could have restricted the looting, guarded munitions sites and borders, and significantly dampened the lawlessness that swept over the country. These and other actions aimed at preempting and reducing opposition probably could have prevented the insurgency from gaining as strong a foothold in Iraq as it now enjoys. (See pp. 139–140.)

OIF May Influence the Behavior of the United States' Future Adversaries in Several Ways

The overwhelming conventional superiority that U.S. forces displayed in OIF may further encourage countries that consider themselves to be potential military adversaries of the United States to seek nuclear weapons in order to ward off submitting to coercion or catastrophic defeat by technologically advanced U.S. military forces. In this respect, OIF may constitute an additional spur to nuclear proliferation in countries such as Iran and North Korea. However, OIF also carried another lesson for potential adversaries: that the United States is willing to take military action, including the takedown of hostile governments, to prevent "rogue" states from acquiring or possessing weapons of mass destruction (WMD). The takedown of Saddam's regime was apparently one of the factors that contributed to Colonel Muammar Qaddafi's decision to abandon Libya's WMD programs. (See pp. 140–142.)

Another major downside lesson that potential adversaries should draw from OIF is that their armor, mechanized, and infantry forces—even if modernized—cannot effectively fight U.S. ground forces so long as U.S. air forces can gain and exploit air supremacy. To cope with this reality, U.S. adversaries can be expected to attach high priority to devising ways to deny U.S. forces air supremacy or, at least, to reduce the adverse effects of that supremacy. Among other approaches, they are likely to seek capabilities that will upgrade the effectiveness of their own air defenses and improve their ability to deny U.S. aircraft the use of proximate air bases. (See pp. 141–142.)

To make aerial attacks less effective and U.S. invasions of their home territories more costly and time-consuming, future adversaries are likely to adopt warfighting strategies that emphasize urban warfare and call for the deployment of heavy, as well as infantry, units in built-up areas, in which they can fight U.S. ground forces from well-prepared positions. (See p. 142.)

Potential adversaries may also draw one other important lesson from OIF: the potential political-military utility of possessing a capability to wage insurgent warfare against U.S. invasion and occupation forces. To develop such a capability, adversaries would organize, train, and equip their ground units for guerrilla-style warfare and position hidden weapon and munitions caches throughout their country. Selected members of the public would also be organized, motivated, and trained to support resistance warfare. Potential adversaries may calculate that the very prospect of becoming bogged down in a protracted guerrilla conflict might serve to deter U.S. leaders from mounting an invasion. If deterrence failed, then protracted insurgency might be a promising strategy for imposing sufficient costs on the United States to force a withdrawal or an agreement to a political settlement acceptable to the enemy's leadership. (See p. 142.)

Indeed, whenever U.S. ground forces become engaged with hostile elements in future conflicts, they must anticipate the possibility of a guerrilla-type response. In such contingencies, the United States will need forces that are organized, trained, equipped, and culturally sensitized for counterinsurgency warfare—attributes and capabilities that, unfortunately, were lacking in many of the U.S. units that first confronted the insurgent resistance in Iraq. (See p. 143.)

Acknowledgments

The author would like to thank Daniel Byman, Andrew Hoehn, Bruce Nardulli, David Ochmanek, Bruce Pirnie, David Shlapak, and Peter Wilson for their helpful comments and suggestions regarding this monograph.

Abbreviations

APC	armored personnel carrier
BBC	British Broadcasting Agency
CAS	close air support
CENTCOM	Central Command
CFLCC	Combined Forces Land Component Commander
CIA	Central Intelligence Agency
CPA	Coalition Provisional Authority
DCI	Director of Central Intelligence
EPW	enemy prisoner of war
FPF	final protective fire
HET	heavy equipment transport
HVA	high-value asset
IAEA	International Atomic Energy Agency
IED	improvised explosive device
IIS	Iraqi Intelligence Service
JCS	Joint Chiefs of Staff
KIA	killed in action

KTO	Kuwait Theater of Operations
LOC	line of communication
MEMRI	Middle East Media and Research Institute
MP	military police
MSR	main supply route
OIF	Operation Iraqi Freedom
ORHA	Office of Reconstruction and Humanitarian Assistance
PSYOPS	psychological operations
RA	Regular Army
RCC	Revolutionary Command Council
RG	Republican Guard
RPG	rocket-propelled grenade
SOUTHCOM	Southern Command
SRG	Special Republican Guard
SSO	Special Security Organization
UK	United Kingdom
UN	United Nations
UNMOVIC	United Nations Monitoring, Verification, and Inspection Commission
USMC	United States Marine Corps
WIA	wounded in action
WMD	weapons of mass destruction

CHAPTER ONE

Introduction

In Operation Iraqi Freedom (OIF), U.S. forces captured Baghdad and deposed Saddam Hussein's regime within a period of less than three weeks. The British units that constituted the other part of the Coalition's invasion force were also able to capture Basra, Iraq's second-largest city, within a similar time period. This document focuses on two questions relating to the rapidity and ease of that military success: (1) Why did the vast majority of Iraqi forces fail to offer significant or effective resistance? and (2) Why did the Iraqi leaders eschew adopting certain defensive measures that would have made the Coalition invasion more difficult and costly?

The Weak Iraqi Resistance

The takedown of Saddam's regime was accomplished without the hard fighting that had been anticipated from Republican Guard units and at the cost of relatively few allied casualties.[1] Between March 19, when the Coalition's attacks commenced, and April 30, 2003, the day before President George W. Bush declared the end of significant combat, U.S. forces lost some 109 personnel killed in action (KIA). Another 542

---

[1]   Lieutenant General David McKiernan, Combined Forces Land Component Commander (CFLCC), expected the fight with the Iraqi Republican Guard units defending Baghdad to be fierce. See Michael R. Gordon and General Bernard E. Trainor, *Cobra II*, New York: Pantheon Books, 2006a, p. 311.

U.S. personnel were wounded in action.[2] British losses were propor-
tionately even lighter—the capture of Basra cost only three United
Kingdom (UK) KIA—in part because of the cautious tactics employed
by the UK commanders.[3]

The forces charged with defending Iraq numbered in excess of
350,000 troops and included some 17 Regular Army divisions (three
of which were armored and three mechanized), six Republican Guard
divisions (three of which were armored and one mechanized), one Special Republican Guard Division, special operations and reserve forces,
and numerous militia units. The force was equipped with over 2,200
tanks, 2,400 armored personnel carriers (APCs), and 4,000 artillery
pieces.[4]

The armored and infantry divisions of the Iraqi Army Regular did
little if any fighting. Most importantly, some of those Iraqi units that
the Coalition had expected to put up the stiffest fight—the Republican Guard armored and infantry divisions and the Special Republican
Guard elements—also offered very little resistance.[5] The only forces
that offered more sustained, although still limited, resistance were the
Fedayeen Saddam and Ba'athist militias and the foreign jihadists who

---

[2] Of the wounded, 116 were returned to duty within 72 hours. See U.S. Department
of Defense, Washington Headquarters, DoD Personnel and Military Casualty Statistics,
"Operation Iraqi Freedom Military Deaths Through April 30, 2003," as of September 2,
2006. Online at http://siadapp.dmdc.osd.mil/personnel/CASUALTY//castop.htm (as of
June 14, 2007).

[3] See Transcript, "The Invasion of Iraq: An Oral History" *Frontline*, PBS, posted March 9,
2004. Hereinafter cited as Frontline Transcript. Online at http://www.pbs.org/wgbh/pages/
frontline/shows/invasion/etc/script.html (as of March 15, 2005).

[4] The size of the regular Iraqi armed forces was estimated at between 330,000 and
430,000 men, including some 50,000 to 80,000 Republican Guard troops. See Colonel
Gregory Fontenot, U.S. Army, Retired, Lieutenant Colonel E. J. Degen, U.S. Army, and
Lieutenant Colonel David Tohn, U.S. Army (Operation Iraqi Freedom Study Group, Office
of the Chief of Staff U.S. Army, Washington, D.C.), *On Point*, Fort Leavenworth, Kansas:
Combat Studies Institute Press, 2004, p. 100.

[5] During OIF, Special Republican Guard elements played no role in combat as maneuver
units. See Charles Duelfer, Special Advisor to the Director of Central Intelligence (DCI),
Comprehensive Report of the Special Adviser to the DCI on Iraq's WMD, September 30, 2004,
Volume I, p. 93.

had come to Iraq for the express purpose of fighting the invaders. In the course of the march up to Baghdad, U.S. ground forces rarely confronted cohesive enemy units of even battalion size.

By the time U.S. forces entered Baghdad, the Iraqi Army had largely dissolved. But formal Iraqi surrenders were comparatively few. Out of a total enemy force of some 350,000, only about 7,000 (2 percent) were taken prisoner by Coalition forces—a fraction of the more than 85,000 Iraqis captured by Coalition forces in the 1991 Gulf War.[6] Not a single organized Iraqi military unit remained intact when major combat ended. All the Iraqis who had survived the war, including those in units that had no contact with Coalition ground forces, had "self-demobilized" by going home.[7]

The Iraqi Failure to Exploit More-Effective Defensive Options

Saddam's defensive deployments and combat strategy proved ineffective as U.S. units rapidly cut through a generally weak Iraqi defense and occupied Baghdad. Surprisingly, the Iraqis failed to employ a number of tactics and defensive measures that would have made the Coalition's invasion more difficult and costly. Among other missed opportunities, the Iraqis failed to

- mine the roads and destroy the many bridges that lay along the routes of the Coalition's advance
- flood the lower Tigris and Euphrates River Valleys and other potential choke points by destroying dams and dikes
- ignite oil fields and other oil facilities, on a wide-scale, as they had done in Kuwait in 1991

---

[6] Stephen T. Hosmer, *Effects of the Coalition Air Campaign Against Iraqi Ground Forces in the Gulf War*, Santa Monica, Calif.: RAND Corporation, MR-305/1-AF, 2002, p. 170.

[7] See Walter B. Slocombe, "To Build an Army," *The Washington Post*, November 5, 2003, p. A29.

- prepare extensive hardened fighting positions and other defenses in urban areas
- deploy a large portion of Iraq's infantry and armored forces in Baghdad, Basra, and the other urban centers to fight in these built-up areas.

Sources

Interviews with former senior Iraqi civilian and military officials, combatant commanders, and enlisted personnel provide authoritative insights into why the Iraqi resistance to the Coalition invasion in spring 2003 was so weak. For purposes of this report, the author has drawn upon two different sources of interviews: (1) former senior Iraqi military officers who were not detained by Coalition forces but who freely submitted to interviews by American and other correspondents, and (2) so-called High Value Detainees, mostly held at Camp Cropper in Baghdad, who were debriefed and interrogated under the supervision of U.S. government personnel. The High Value Detainees included Saddam Hussein and many of the key political and military officials who populated his regime and senior officer corps. Much of the substance of these governmental interrogations was published on September 30, 2004, in Charles Duelfer's *Comprehensive Report of the Special Adviser to the DCI on Iraq's WMD*. However, the interrogation reports containing the statements of the various High Value Detainees remain classified.

Caution must be exercised in weighing testimony from participants in a losing cause. There is the risk that the sources will present their own actions in a self-serving light and blame others for Iraq's poor military showing and easy defeat. Statements by High Value Detainees about their own role in the Iraqi regime and their own possible liability for its nefarious activities must be viewed with particular caution, because the prospect of prosecution is likely to have constrained the detainee's candor and to have otherwise influenced their answers. Moreover, some detainee testimony may have been contaminated by the fact that the Iraqis held at Camp Cropper were able to interact freely among themselves and exchange information about the questions they had been asked and the answers they had tendered.[8]

Even taking account of these cautionary considerations, the author believes that the statements by Iraqi sources concerning the issues addressed in this report are, by and large, credible. First, this study does not focus on topics (such as the past use of weapons of mass destruction [WMD], abuse of human rights, and responsibility for aggression) that are likely to be subjects of future criminal trials. Second, there is a consistency between the information freely provided by Iraqi sources to the news media and the information extracted from High Value Detainees by official interrogators.[9] Third, the interviews of Iraqi rank-and-file soldiers tend to confirm the statements of the senior officers. Finally, the information the Iraqi sources presented is entirely consistent with the Iraqi military and diplomatic behavior observed during the period leading up to OIF and the Iraqi battlefield performance during the course of the conflict that followed.

Organization of the Monograph

The analysis presented in the following chapters examines the various causes for the surprisingly vulnerable Iraqi defensive posture at the start of OIF and for the extraordinarily weak Iraqi resistance to the Coalition invasion. The report examines the following key factors that both singly and in combination produced the rapid Iraqi collapse:

- Saddam's strategic miscalculations, which were of great importance in that all key decisions relating to the defense of Iraq rested with the Iraqi leader

---

[8]   Duelfer (2004), p. 2.

[9]   One reporter who interviewed a number of Iraqi officers after the war, found that "the close parallels among experiences described by military leaders from field units, headquarters, divisions, and special forces assigned to a wide variety of locations buttressed their credibility" (Molly Moore, "A Foe That Collapsed from Within," *The Washington Post*, July 20, 2003, p. A1).

- the consequences of Saddam's preoccupation with internal threats to his person and regime
- the shortcomings in strategy, leadership, command and control, coordination, battlefield positioning, situational awareness, and training that plagued the Iraqi forces, and the old equipment provided to those forces
- the poor initial motivation and morale of the vast majority of the officers and enlisted personnel serving in the Regular Army and Republican Guard, and the damaging effects of U.S. air strikes on that morale
- the superior attributes of U.S. and other Coalition military forces, particularly their training, mobility, and ability to apply accurate firepower.

The monograph concludes with a discussion of why U.S. decision-makers should be careful about the lessons they draw from OIF, how OIF set the stage for the insurgency that followed, and how OIF may influence the calculations and behavior of the United States' future adversaries.

CHAPTER TWO

Saddam Made Strategic Miscalculations

That Saddam Hussein seriously miscalculated the prospects of conflict with the United States, and the nature and intensity of the attacks that Iraq might face, should war come about, was a major reason Iraq failed to adopt the more robust defensive measures that could have made the Coalition invasion more difficult and costly. Saddam had a propensity for such miscalculation, stemming in large part from his dysfunctional personality and cognitive traits, his limited grasp of international and military affairs, and the cultures of "fear" and "lying" that his rule engendered, which discouraged the offer of countervailing advice and information from intimidated subordinates. Saddam's misjudgments about Coalition intentions and capabilities importantly shaped Iraqi behavior both before and during the 2003 conflict.

Saddam Was the Only Decisionmaker Who Mattered

Because Saddam Hussein was the dominant decisionmaker in Iraq, these miscalculations shaped Iraq's political-military responses to the crisis over Iraq's presumed possession of WMD and the impending Coalition attack.

Saddam's writ in Iraq was both sweeping and absolute. He formally controlled every state, administrative, Ba'ath Party, and military hierarchy in the country: He simultaneously held the posts of President, Prime Minister, Chairman of the Revolutionary Command Council (RCC), General Secretary of the Ba'ath Party, and Commander in Chief of the Armed Forces.[1]

Saddam's major strategic decisions were made by fiat, often without consultation or reflection. He was prone to indulge in the micro-management of all aspects of government. This propensity was most evident in the early period of his rule. After the mid-1990s, when Saddam became more security-conscious and reclusive (he took to writing novels), he had less immediate contact with the government.[2] During this later period, Saddam relied increasingly on verbal instructions passed to a network of family and other trusted subordinates to administer Iraq's affairs. When the Iraqi leader failed to provide specific guidance on a matter, his subordinates were forced to act "upon what they perceived to be indirect or implied orders from him."[3]

But Saddam's bent for micromanagement—particularly in military and security areas—never disappeared and was still evident in the final months of his rule. He maintained command over Iraq's armed forces, militias, and intelligence services, and exercised direct authority over the plans and operations of these organizations. Reporting directly to Saddam—or to Saddam through his two sons, Qusay and Uday, or through other loyal and pliable subordinate officials—were the Republican Guard (RG), the Special Republican Guard (SRG), the Regular Army (RA), the Fedayeen Saddam militia, the Ba'athist militia, the Al Quds Army, and Iraq's four intelligence agencies.[4]

According to the former Iraqi Minister of Defense, Staff General Sultan Hashim Ahmad Al Ta'i, Saddam addressed military and military-industrialization issues directly with the Minister of Defense or the Minister of Military Industrialization without the intermediate filter of any Cabinet, RCC, or other governmental discussion. However, these officials exercised little or no independent authority. Except for issues involving the Republican Guard, over which he had

---

[1] Duelfer (2004), p. 5.

[2] After 1998, Saddam manifested less grasp of details and would often come to ministers' meetings unprepared. See Duelfer (2004), pp. 9 and 12.

[3] Duelfer (2004), p. 5.

[4] Duelfer (2004), pp. 5 and 16.

no authority, the Iraqi Minister of Defense is said to have forwarded all military matters of any significance to Saddam for his consideration and approval.[5] Issues relating to the Republican Guard were discussed directly by Saddam with his son Qusay, who had overall supervision of the Republican Guard, and the Republican Guard Chief-of-Staff.[6] In addition, Saddam was also prone to giving instructions directly to subordinate battlefield commanders.

Saddam's Decisionmaking Was Seriously Flawed

Saddam's propensity for strategic miscalculation can be attributed to his congenital optimism, excessive self-confidence, and poor understanding of international and military affairs. The erroneous assumptions underlying his decisions went unchallenged because Saddam was surrounded by equally uninformed sycophants and other subordinates who were fearful of conveying bad news or telling him truths that they believed he did not want to hear. The climate of fear Saddam engendered gave rise to a "culture of lying," whereby senior military officers routinely misled Saddam about the readiness and fighting will of their forces.

Saddam's Decisions Were Distorted by Optimism and Overweening Self-Confidence

Saddam's penchant for miscalculation can be traced in part to his congenital optimism. One scholar, Amatzia Baram, has described Saddam as a man who "always believes that things are going to turn out in his favor, no matter how bad they might look to others." This unabated optimism was shaped by the Iraqi leader's "life of achievements in the face of overwhelming odds." Saddam believed his mother had attempted to abort him and that "his very birth was his first victory in a struggle to survive." According to Baram, Saddam's "remarkable success in rising

---

[5] Duelfer (2004), p. 16.

[6] This according to the testimony of former Iraqi Minister of Foreign Affairs and later Deputy Prime Minister Tariq Aziz. See Duelfer (2004), p. 16.

to the top and staying in power despite all of his initial disadvantages had convinced him that he was marked out by destiny."[7]

That he was able to survive potentially fatal mistakes—such as the invasions of Iran and Kuwait—only served to fuel his self-confidence. Indeed, according to Saddam's former presidential office director, Hamid Yusif Hammadi, "after the Iran-Iraq War, Saddam was intoxicated with conceit. He believed he was unbeatable."[8] Incongruously, Saddam persistently claimed both privately and publicly that the 1991 Persian Gulf War had ended in an Iraqi victory.[9]

Saddam's megalomania was manifest in his sometimes-stated aspiration "to be remembered as a ruler who had been as significant to Iraq as Hammurabi, Nebuchadnezzar and Salah-al-Din [Saladin]." As a consequence, he was prone to manage his present affairs always with a view to how his actions might be viewed by future generations.[10]

Moreover, when facing potential crises, Saddam had a propensity to willfully distort facts and interpret events to fit his preconceived notions. Once Saddam determined how he expected and wanted a situation to evolve, he tended to disregard evidence and interpretations that might undercut his optimistic scenario and focused only on information and explanations that would support what he wanted to be true. Thus, he invariably interpreted "all of the available data to conform to what would be best for him."[11] These propensities led Saddam to take major risks.

---

[7] See Amatzia Baram, "Would Saddam Husayn Abdicate?" Washington, D.C.: The Brookings Institution, Iraq Memo No. 9, February 4, 2003, pp. 1–2.

[8] Hammadi was Secretary of the President and presidential office director, 1982–1991. Duelfer (2004), p. 26.

[9] Saddam tended to see his life as a "relentless struggle against overwhelming odds, but carried out with courage, perseverance and dignity." In the context of the "Mother of All Battles"—Saddam's name for the 1991 Persian Gulf War—"Saddam showed a stubbornness arising from such a mindset and a refusal to accept conventional definitions of defeat." In Saddam's reckoning, even a hollow victory was a "real one" (Duelfer, 2004, p. 20).

[10] Duelfer (2004), p. 22.

[11] Kenneth M. Pollack, *The Threatening Storm: The Case for Invading Iraq*, New York: Random House, 2002b, p. 254.

Saddam Had a Limited Grasp of International and Military Affairs

Saddam's interests and experience had provided him with only a very limited understanding of the outside world. Saddam rarely traveled abroad, and his foreign-affairs interests focused primarily on Arab nations. According to the assessment of his former Minister of Foreign Affairs and later, Deputy Prime Minister, Tariq Aziz, Saddam "lacked a full grasp of international affairs":

> Saddam perceived Iraqi foreign policy through the prism of the Arab world and Arabic language. He listened to the Arabic services of Voice of America and the BBC, and his press officers would read him translations of foreign media, but he appeared more interested in books and topics about the Arab world.[12]

Saddam's insight about the outside world was apparently also gleaned from motion pictures. He watched classic U.S. movies and told a U.S. interviewer that he relied on movies to understand Western culture.[13]

Saddam's understanding of the United States was clouded at best. He failed to understand U.S. interests and the internal and external drivers that shaped U.S. policy. For example, he completely misread the import of September 11, 2001 (9/11) as it might influence U.S. attitudes toward Iraq. He was the only Arab leader who failed to express sympathy to the American people and to condemn the terrorist attacks. By failing to do so, Saddam's colleagues believed he missed a major opportunity to reduce tensions with the United States. Instead, he "reinforced U.S. suspicions about his connections to Al Qa'ida and certified Iraq's credentials as a rogue state."[14]

---

[12]   Duelfer (2004), p. 8.

[13]   Duelfer (2004), p. 8.

[14]   Saddam reportedly rejected advice from his Cabinet to offer condolences to the United States. According to the Duelfer report, "he told his ministers that after all the hardships the Iraqi people had suffered under sanctions he could not extend official condolences to the United States, the government most responsible for blocking sanctions relief. From a practical standpoint, Saddam probably also believed—mistakenly—that his behavior toward the

Saddam viewed Iran as more of a threat to Iraqi security than he did the United States.[15] He and other senior Iraqi officials looked upon Iran as Iraq's "abiding enemy" and sought to keep the threat posed by Tehran in check. In addition to possible invasion, Saddam worried that Iranian infiltrators might foment internal unrest in the country.[16] Saddam's interest in Iraq's development of WMD was driven in part by the growth of Iranian weapons capabilities. Saddam also worried that Israel might be encouraged to attack Iraq if it knew that Iraq did not possess WMD.[17] Because of his concerns about Iran and Israel, Saddam was loath to publicly proclaim that Iraq no longer possessed WMD. As the Duelfer report points out,

> [t]his led to a difficult balancing act between the need to disarm to achieve sanctions relief while at the same time retaining a strategic deterrent. The Regime never resolved the contradiction inherent in this approach. Ultimately, foreign perceptions of these tensions contributed to the destruction of the Regime.[18]

Some high-ranking Iraqi detainees also attributed Saddam's unwillingness to categorically disavow possession of WMD to his fear that he would lose face with his Arab neighbors, such as Saudi Arabia,

---

United States was of little consequence, as sanctions were on the verge of collapse" (Duelfer, 2004, pp. 33 and 57).

[15] During the 1990s, Saddam and members of his inner circle considered a full-scale invasion of Iraq by American forces "to be the most dangerous potential threat to unseating the Regime, although Saddam rated the probability of an invasion as very low." According to Tariq Aziz, "Saddam did not consider the United States a natural adversary, as he did Iran and Israel, and he hoped that Iraq might again enjoy improved relations with the United States. . . ." (Duelfer, 2004, p. 31).

[16] See Duelfer (2004), pp. 29–30, 72.

[17] See Kevin M. Woods with Michael R. Pease, Mark E. Stout, Williamson Murray, and James G. Lacey, *Iraqi Perspectives Project: A View of Operation Iraqi Freedom from Saddam's Senior Leadership*, Norfolk, Va.: U.S. Joint Forces Command, Joint Center for Operational Analysis and Lessons Learned, 2006, p. 311. The study's findings are based on "dozens of interviews with senior Iraqi military and political leaders" and an analysis of "thousands of official Iraqi documents."

[18] See Duelfer (2004), p. 34.

Kuwait, and the United Arab Emirates, that paid him deference because they thought he had weapons of mass destruction. Senior Iraqi generals offered a similar view, stating that Saddam "had an inferiority complex" and "wanted the whole region to look at him as a grand leader." But the generals also believed that "during the period when the Americans were massing troops in Kuwait, he wanted to deter the prospect of war."[19] By this account, Saddam failed to grasp until it was too late that the U.S. perception that Iraq possessed WMD was a spur to invasion, not a deterrent to one.

Saddam was also largely unschooled in military affairs. Iraqi general officers captured during the 1991 Gulf War spoke disparagingly of Saddam's military knowledge. They characterized the Iraqi leader as a "gambler" lacking in military judgment and experience. As one senior Iraqi officer commenting on the Iraqi defeat put it: "Saddam has never worn combat boots, dug a foxhole, done PT [physical training], or lived through what soldiers live through. Yet he pretends to lead the military, and we can see the results."[20]

Saddam's Advisers Were Uninformed, Timid, and Sycophantic

Saddam's decisionmaking was further distorted by his exposure to little countervailing information or opinion. Because his intelligence services focused in the main on internal threats, they were not positioned well to provide Saddam with a "comprehensive or objective picture of his strategic situation."[21]

The Iraqi leader's key advisers were both loath to offer opinions contrary to Saddam's and largely untutored themselves in international and military affairs. The members of the Committee of Four (the Quartet)—who supposedly constituted Saddam's most senior advisory group—"had only a limited and hazy view of the United States, its

---

[19] See Steve Coll, "Hussein Was Sure of Own Survival; Aide Says Confusion Reigned on Eve of War," *The Washington Post*, November 3, 2003, p. A1.

[20] Hosmer (2002), p. 86.

[21] Pollack (2002b), p. 255.

interests, and how policy was formed and driven in Washington."[22] Moreover, the Quartet offered no proactive advice or recommendations contrary to what the Quartet members perceived to be Saddam's predisposition on issues. As a consequence, the Quartet failed to have a significant effect on Saddam's policy on any significant matter.[23]

Saddam employed violence and patronage as administrative methods for ensuring loyalty and compliance with his orders and for repressing criticism of any sort, helpful or not.[24] His willingness to order the jailing or execution of those he thought disloyal was in the forefront of the minds of his subordinates. As a result, Saddam came to be surrounded by sycophantic military and civilian officials who would tell the Iraqi leader only what they thought he wanted to hear. All were aware of Saddam's penchant for punishing the bearers of bad news and, in particular, persons who had had the temerity to disagree with him. As Jerrold Post, a long-term government psychologist and expert on Saddam, put it: "One criticizes a policy or decision of Saddam's at great peril[,] for to criticize Saddam is to be disloyal, and to be disloyal is to lose one's job or one's life."[25]

Interviews with Saddam's key aides underscore the extent to which their advice was constrained by their fear of Saddam and their

---

[22] Tariq Aziz, who had some grounding in international affairs and was a member of the Quartet, constituted a partial exception to this statement. However, "at no stage did the Quartet demonstrate a strategic concept of what the U.S. wanted with Iraq, where common ground and differences really lay, and the nature of the challenge the U.S. or Coalition presented. Nor did they have a strategy for dealing with the West, apart from tactical games at the UN." The other members of the Quartet were 'Izzat Ibrahim Al Duri, Taha Yasin Ramadan Al Jizrawi, and 'Ali Hasan Al Majid. Duelfer (2004), pp. 6 and 71.

[23] Duelfer (2004), pp. 70–71.

[24] Duelfer (2004), pp. 8–9 and 12. Toby Dodge writes that, on a broader scale, Saddam "used extreme levels of violence and the powers of patronage delivered by oil wealth to co-opt or break any independent vestiges of civil society" in Iraq. "Autonomous collective societal structures beyond the control of the state simply [did] not exist. In their place, society came to be dominated by aspects of the 'shadow state,' flexible networks of patronage and violence that were used to reshape Iraqi society in the image of Saddam Hussein and his regime" (Toby Dodge, *Inventing Iraq: The Failure of Nation Building and a History Denied*, New York: Columbia University Press, 2003, p. 159).

[25] Quoted in Pollack (2002b), p. 254.

concern that they might lose the patronage and appearance of power he provided them. At the meetings of the RCC, which was purported to be Iraq's highest-ranking decisionmaking body, Saddam made all the decisions and "there was never any objection to his decisions."[26] One of Saddam's cousins and most trusted subordinates, 'Ali Hasan Al Majid (Chemical Ali) indicated that he knew of no instance when anyone had brought bad news to Saddam.[27] According to the former Deputy Prime Minister and Minister of Military Industrialization, Abd-al-Tawab 'Abdallah Al Mullah Huwaysh, no minister at a Cabinet meeting would ever argue against Saddam's stated position, because it would be "unforgivable. It would be suicide."[28]

The muting of contrary opinion had a pernicious effect on Iraqi policies. One of Saddam's Vice Presidents, Taha Yasin Ramadan Al Jizrawi, reports that, from late 2002 onward, he was convinced that Iraqi policy toward the United States and the United Nations (UN) was taking the country toward a disastrous war. However, he reports that he was intimidated from pushing the issue with Saddam: "I couldn't convince Saddam that an attack was coming[;] I didn't try that hard. He was monitoring my performance in managing [UN] inspectors."[29]

Saddam Had a Record of Strategic Blunders

Saddam had demonstrated a propensity for strategic blundering in his management of Iraq's earlier wars.

In 1980, Saddam ordered Iraqi forces to mount an incursion into Iran, mistakenly believing that a short "blitzkrieg" to take and hold territory in southern Iran would be sufficient to coerce concessions from the Khomeni regime and possibly cause its ouster. Among other objectives, Saddam sought to gain total control of the Shatt al-Arab

---

[26] This according to Muhammad Hamzah Al Zubaydi, a former member of the RCC. See Duelfer (2004), pp. 5 and 14.

[27] Duelfer (2004), p. 11.

[28] Duelfer (2004), p. 19.

[29] Duelfer (2004), p. 19.

waterway (Iraq's primary outlet to the Persian Gulf) and to force Iran's revolutionary leaders to desist from their subversive activities among the Iraq's Shia population that Saddam believed were aimed at the overthrow of his regime.[30]

Saddam erroneously believed that any Iranian opposition to the invasion would be light and short-lived. He assumed that Iraq's more numerous armored and infantry forces in the region would rapidly overwhelm an Iranian military establishment that had been severely weakened by purges and desertions. However, the Iraqi invasion was poorly planned and inadequately prepared, and the Iranian resistance proved stronger than anticipated. The Iraqi forces invading Iran moved at an overly deliberate pace and failed to exploit the element of surprise that they had initially achieved. The slow pace of the advance saved the Iranians from a possible catastrophic loss of territory and oil-production facilities and gave the Tehran regime precious time to reorganize, regroup, and move reinforcements to the front.[31] Rather than prompting the quick accommodation Saddam hoped for, the Iranian authorities capitalized on the Iraqi attack to consolidate their hold on power, mobilize additional military forces, and embark on an eight-year war of attrition that exacted a significant toll on Iraq.[32]

Saddam invaded Kuwait in 1990 to seize that country's oil fields and oil facilities and thereby ease Iraq's economic difficulties stemming from the heavy burden of debt it had accumulated during the Iran-Iraq War. Resolving long-standing irredentist grievances was a secondary

---

[30] Saddam apparently also believed that attacking Iran would enhance his prestige with other Arab leaders who feared the Iranian leader's, Ayatollah Khomeni's, influence. Saddam may also have hoped to seize control of all of Khuzestan Province, which contained most of Iran's oil wells and oil-production facilities. See Duelfer (2004), p. 41, and Kenneth M. Pollack, *Arabs At War*, Lincoln: University of Nebraska Press, 2002a, pp. 182–184.

[31] Saddam offered to voluntarily halt the Iraqi advance after only two weeks of fighting. This offer, however, seems to have been a ploy to garner time to regroup Iraqi forces before resuming the offensive. See Efraim Karsh and Inari Rautsi, *Saddam Hussein*, New York: The Free Press, 1991, p. 149, and Pollack (2002a), pp. 186–193.

[32] The war is estimated to have cost Iraq some 375,000 casualties, 60,000 prisoners, and $150 billion. See Duelfer (2004), p. 41.

motivation in that Saddam viewed Kuwait as rightfully the 19th province of Iraq.[33]

In deciding to invade, Saddam erroneously miscalculated that the United States would not go to war over Kuwait. He was also unprepared for the harsh reaction from the other permanent members of the UN Security Council, particularly the Soviet Union, and was also "surprised by the condemnation of fellow Arab leaders[,] many of whom he knew detested the Kuwaitis."[34]

By limiting his offense to Kuwait, Saddam eschewed the option—clearly available to Iraq at the time-to also overrun Saudi Arabia and the Persian Gulf sheikdoms, which would have given Iraq control over most of the world's petroleum production and provided Saddam with enormous bargaining leverage over the West. Ironically, to garner the forces needed to defend his conquest of Kuwait, Saddam found it necessary to secure Iraq's northeastern flank by signing a peace agreement with Iran that forfeited all the territorial gains Iraq had made in the costly Iran-Iraq War.[35] Saddam also erred in the Gulf War by refusing to withdraw from Kuwait under generally advantageous terms when confronted with the prospect of an air and ground war with the United States and its Coalition partners.

Saddam's willingness to risk a military confrontation with the United States over Kuwait rested on several key miscalculations: that the United States would not go to war over Kuwait, that Iraq would be able to impose unacceptable casualties on American forces, that the Coalition's resolve to force Iraq's withdrawal from Kuwait would weaken over time, that Coalition airpower would not be a decisive factor in the conflict, and that the tactics that Iraq used against Iran

---

[33] While Saddam had planned for an invasion some weeks beforehand, "the impulsive decision to invade in August 1990 was precipitated by what Saddam chose to perceive as Kuwait's arrogance in negotiations over disputed drilling along the common border" (Duelfer, 2004, p. 42).

[34] Duelfer (2004), p. 42.

[35] Roland Dannreuther, *The Gulf Conflict: A Political and Strategic Analysis*, Adelphi Paper 264, London: International Institute for Strategic Studies, Winter 1991–1992, p. 31.

would also succeed against Coalition forces.[36] Several of Saddam's Gulf War misperceptions carried over to 2003 and contributed to his miscalculations about OIF.

Saddam Made Several Strategic Miscalculations in 2003

According to the testimony of Saddam's former high-ranking aides, the Iraqi leader profoundly misread the situation Iraq faced in late 2002 and early 2003. Among other miscalculations, the aides report that Saddam believed that (1) the United States would not attack Iraq, (2) if the United States did attack, it would be by air and not by ground invasion, and, finally, (3) if the United States did invade, Iraqi forces by employing the strategy Saddam had devised, would be capable of forcing the United States to accept a political settlement that left his regime in power. These erroneous assumptions stemmed in large part from the shortcomings in Saddam's decisionmaking discussed above and from the Iraqi leader's penchant for relying on misleading historical analogies as guides for likely future U.S. behavior.

War Could Be Avoided

Saddam apparently believed, until early 2003, that war with the United States could be avoided. Saddam's misreading of U.S. interests and objectives with regard to his regime was a key reason for this belief. His subordinates report that Saddam had told them on numerous occasions that following the 1991 war, the "United States had achieved all it wanted in the Gulf." According to detainee interviews, "by late 2002 Saddam had persuaded himself, just as he did in 1991, that the United States would not attack Iraq because it already had achieved its objective of establishing a military presence in the region."[37]

---

[36] Hosmer (2002), pp. 10–12.

[37] This and other testimony belie Saddam's claim during interrogation that "it was clear to him, some four months before the war, that hostilities were inevitable." See Duelfer (2004), p. 32.

Saddam also overestimated what France, China, and Russia might do in the United Nations Security Council to constrain a U.S. attack.[38] He believed that time was on his side and that the United States would never be allowed to attack.[39]

Tariq Aziz reportedly told his U.S. interrogators that Russian and French intermediaries had persuaded Saddam that "he might yet avoid a war that would end his regime, despite ample evidence to the contrary."[40] According to Aziz's account, the French and Russian intermediaries repeatedly assured Saddam during meetings in late 2002 and early 2003 "that they would block a U.S.-led war through delays and vetoes at the U.N. Security Council."[41]

Finally, Saddam believed that he could forestall any attacks by demonstrating that Iraq possessed no WMD and was fully cooperating with United Nations Monitoring, Verification, and Inspection Commission (UNMOVIC) inspections. He apparently calculated that Iraq's cooperation with UNMOVIC would not only remove a *causus belli* but would also bring sanctions to an end. In December 2002, Saddam assembled senior Iraqi officials and directed them to cooperate completely with inspectors. He ordered the Republican Guard, which in earlier years had obstructed inspections, to prepare to have an "open house" for UNMOVIC inspectors "day and night."[42] This zeal to cooperate was readily apparent to the weapons inspectors. Hans Blix, the executive director of UNMOVIC, reports that in early 2003, the "Iraqis had become much more active-even frantic-in their cooperation."[43]

---

[38] Duelfer (2004), p. 49.

[39] Duelfer (2004), p. 67.

[40] Aziz described the man he had long served as a "distracted, distrustful despot" by the eve of the war. See Coll (2003).

[41] Both the French and the Russian governments denied having conveyed the messages alleged to them. See "France Denies Coaxing Saddam on Invasion," Associated Press, November 4, 2003. Online at http://www.lasvegassun.com/sunbin/stories/text/2003/nov/04/110405167/html (as of February 27, 2004).

[42] Duelfer (2004), p. 63.

[43] Hans Blix, *Disarming Iraq*, New York: Pantheon Books, 2004, p. 196.

Iraq's energetic public diplomacy in the weeks before the March 19th attack suggests that Saddam had hopes of generating political pressures within the international community that would stave off a U.S.-led onslaught. As late as March 15, the Iraqi Foreign Ministry invited the UN's two chief weapons inspectors to travel to Iraq "at the earliest possible date" to discuss "means to speed up joint cooperation in all fields." To demonstrate its willingness to cooperate, Iraq offered the names of several dozen Iraqi scientists and other persons who had participated in the destruction of WMD, invited UN inspectors to conduct tests at sites where chemical or biological agents were said to have been dumped or destroyed, and continued to flatten the Al Samoud-2 missiles that the UN had found to exceed permitted range limits.[44]

In the days preceding the outbreak of hostilities, top Iraqi intelligence officials—almost certainly with Saddam's concurrence—reportedly attempted to open a secret communication channel, using a Lebanese-American businessman as an intermediary with the Bush administration to avoid war. Among other inducements, the Iraqis reportedly told their intermediary to tell his American contacts that Iraq would (1) allow U.S. troops and experts to conduct an independent search so as to prove that Iraq possessed no weapons of mass destruction, (2) hand over a man accused of being involved in the World Trade Center bombing of 1993 who was being held in Iraq, and (3) hold elections.[45]

Even after hostilities commenced, Iraqi officials were appealing for diplomatic action to stop the Coalition attacks. Vice President Taha Yassin Ramadan Al Jizrawi on March 23 called on the United Nations to intervene and halt the fighting. "Ramadan appealed to Arab governments to press for diplomacy. He and other officials appeared to take

---

[44] For a description of the various measures Iraq employed to buttress its claim that it no longer had weapons of mass destruction, see Rajiv Chandrasekaran, "Iraq Seeks Meeting With U.N. Inspectors," *The Washington Post*, March 16, 2003, p. A14, and Duelfer (2004), pp. 63–64.

[45] See James Risen, "Baghdad Scrambled to Offer Deal to U.S. as War Loomed," *The New York Times*, November 5, 2003, and "Bush Aides Play Down Effort to Avert War at Last Minute," *The New York Times*, November 7, 2003.

heart from footage of protests across the Arab world, and chastised Arab leaders for blocking antiwar demonstrations."[46]

Any Attacks Would Be Limited: Iraq Would Not Be Invaded

Even if war could not be avoided, Saddam was apparently convinced that American forces would not invade Iraq.[47] According to a former senior Ba'ath Party member, Saddam was convinced that a show of force would be sufficient to deter an invasion as the United States would seek to avoid another Vietnam and the casualties that an invasion would entail.[48] Saddam was reinforced in this view by the U.S. failure to march on Baghdad at the close of the 1991 Gulf War, which he attributed to an American unwillingness to incur additional casualties.[49] Commenting on Saddam's overconfidence about U.S. casualty sensitivity, Tariq Aziz had the following exchange with his debriefer:

> Aziz: A few weeks before the attacks, Saddam thought the U.S. would not use ground forces; he thought that you would only use your air force.
>
> Debriefer: Wasn't he aware of the buildup of forces in the region?
>
> Aziz: Of course he was aware, it was all over the television screen. He thought they would not fight a ground war because it would be too costly to the Americans. He was overconfident. He was clever, but his calculations were poor. It wasn't that he wasn't

---

[46] Anthony Shadid, "Iraqi Officials Emerge, Bolstered by U.S. Setbacks," *The Washington Post*, March 24, 2003a, p. A21.

[47] See Mark Hosenball, "Iraq: What in the World Was Saddam Thinking?" *Newsweek*, September 15, 2003, p. 8. Saddam's views were reported to *Newsweek* by U.S. officials who were familiar with the accounts of Saddam's thinking provided to American interrogators by some of the former Iraqi leader's associates. Also see Duelfer (2004), p. 31.

[48] Duelfer (2004), p. 67.

[49] See Woods et al. (2006), p. 16.

receiving the information. It was right there on television, but he didn't understand international relations perfectly.[50]

Instead of an invasion, Saddam believed that President Bush would call for a "low-risk bombing campaign" similar to that employed by the Clinton administration against Iraq in Operation Desert Fox and against the former Federal Republic of Yugoslavia in Operation Allied Force.[51] Moreover, he believed that any bombing campaign would probably be short-lived, because France, Germany, Russia, and China would pressure the United States to "retreat from this course," and leave "Saddam still in power."[52] Even after U.S. forces had assembled on Iraq's border with Kuwait, "Saddam, recalling the first gulf war, thought U.S. ground forces would only go after suspected unconventional weapons sites, Scud missile launchers and military bases."[53]

His Regime Would Survive an Invasion

Finally, even if the United States were to invade Iraq, Saddam believed that Iraqi forces, using the strategy he had designed, would be able to force the United States to settle for a political solution that would leave his regime in place. In holding to this view, Saddam made several erroneous assumptions.

First, he assumed that the Iraqi military would be motivated and capable of mounting an effective, protracted defense. Saddam was encouraged in this belief by senior officers and civilian officials throughout the chain of command who consistently and blatantly lied to him about the readiness and fighting will of the Iraqi armed forces.[54] A culture of lying to superiors had grown in the Iraqi officer corps during the 1990s, driven by fear of Saddam and his regime and by

---

[50] Quoted in Duelfer (2004), p. 67.

[51] According to some Iraqi officials, Saddam believed that the Desert Fox–type air strikes would be the "worst" form of pressure he could expect to undergo from the United States. See Duelfer (2004), p. 49.

[52] Hosenball (2003), p. 8, and Duelfer (2004), pp. 32 and 49.

[53] Hosenball (2003), p. 8.

[54] Duelfer (2004), p. 11.

the inability of the military to achieve results as resources deteriorated under sanctions imposed by the United Nations.[55]

General Ghanem Abdullah Azawi, an engineer in the Iraqi air defense command, described examples of the "culture of self-deception in which soldiers and officers consistently lied to one another about everything from the condition of their equipment to the presence of U.S. forces inside Baghdad":

> There has been practically no air defense since 1991. . . . Nobody rebuilt it. We didn't receive any new weapons. TV broadcasts boasting of scientists' modifications to Iraqi air defense missiles were "lies, all lies." . . . "People were lying to Saddam and Saddam was believing them or deceiving himself." Whenever anyone would ask about the state of their equipment, "we would always say, very good. . . . It was all lies, because if you told the truth . . . you'd be in trouble. . . . One lied to the other from the first lieutenant up until it reached Saddam. Even Saddam Hussein was lying to himself."[56]

Saddam was also deceived about the status of some of his longer-term weapon-development programs. General Yasin Mohammad Taha Joubouri, a Regular Army artillery specialist, explained how he and his colleagues had systematically deceived Saddam about the status of a 210-millimeter (mm) cannon the Iraqi leader had ordered them to build. Fully aware that the cannon they had designed would never work, General Joubouri and the other artillery specialists assigned to work on the weapon nevertheless built a full-scale model of the non-functional weapon and submitted fake performance records to convince Saddam that the project was on track. As General Joubouri described the situation: "No one could tell him it couldn't work. . . . He was giving us awards and presents."[57]

---

[55] Duelfer (2004), p. 11.

[56] See William Branigin, "A Brief, Bitter War for Iraq's Military Officers," *The Washington Post*, April 27, 2003, p. A25.

[57] Moore (2003), p. A1.

Few officers or officials were willing to risk conveying to Saddam the true state of their unit's morale and readiness. Even Saddam's son Qusay, who had been trusted with the supervision of all Iraqi Republican Guard forces, was keen to provide Saddam with good news. Qusay "lived in fear of incurring Saddam's displeasure and optimistically exaggerated information that he gave Saddam." In late 2002, he audaciously boasted to his father, "we are ten times more powerful than in 1991."[58]

In the run-up to the war, Saddam met with numerous commanders of various Iraqi units. In each and every meeting, there was a statement from the commander asserting that his unit was ready and willing to fight. The publicity often accorded these ritualistic ceremonies no doubt aimed to reassure the Iraqi public and deter military action by the United States.[59] But even in Saddam's private meetings with his senior officers, similar expressions of resolve and readiness to fight were consistently tendered. Saddam no longer sought "ground truth" about the actual status of Iraq's forces as he once had by visiting units and asking pointed questions. Instead, he relied on the reports from officers who deliberately misled him out of fear of losing their positions and even their lives.[60]

Second, Saddam believed that the Iraqi people would not stand to be occupied or conquered by the United States and would rise up and attack any American or other Coalition invaders. According to the former Minister of Defense, Staff General Sultan Hashim Ahmad Al Ta'i, Saddam "thought that the people would, of their own accord, take to the streets and fight with light arms, and that this would deter

---

[58] The then Deputy Prime Minister and Minister of Military Industrialization, Huwaysh, who was present at the meeting, claims that he immediately disagreed with Qusay, saying "Actually, we are 100 times weaker than in 1991, because the people are not ready to fight." Hawaysh reports that Saddam did not respond, but Qusay was angry because Huwaysh had contradicted him. If Huwaysh's account is true, it constitutes one of the rare times when Saddam was given bad news. Duelfer (2004), p. 22.

[59] For a description of the Saddam-military meetings, see Neiel MacFarquhar, "Hussein, in Rallying His Military, Also Shows Iraqis a Defiant Face," *The New York Times*, March 7, 2005, p. 1.

[60] Duelfer (2004), p. 11.

the U.S. forces from entering the cities."[61] Saddam's mistaken conceit that the Iraqi population supported his regime—he had won a referendum on his rule by an overwhelming margin in 2002—apparently underlay this assumption.[62]

Third, Saddam calculated that the robust defense he expected to be mounted by the Iraqi military and populace would exact an unacceptable level of U.S. casualties. He assumed that the specter of large numbers of American casualties and significant U.S.-caused collateral damage would stimulate sufficient international and American domestic anti-war pressures to force the United States to halt its military action and negotiate a political solution.[63]

According to a senior Iraqi official, Saddam believed that Iraqi forces would be capable of holding off any U.S. invaders "for at least a month" and that U.S. forces would not penetrate as far as Baghdad.[64] He may have also believed that even a shorter defense could force a political settlement. This expectation may explain why just before the war began, Saddam told his generals to "hold the Coalition for eight days and leave the rest to him."[65] A former Iraqi general reports that Saddam, almost to the end of the 2003 conflict, clung to the belief that he could "solve the problem politically, as he had done at the end of the 1991 Gulf War."[66]

The U.S. withdrawals from Vietnam, Lebanon, and Somalia apparently convinced Saddam that the United States could not politi-

---

[61] Duelfer (2004), p. 67.

[62] In this pseudo-election, every one of the nation's 11.5 million eligible voters voted to keep Saddam as president. See "Ba'ath Party Entrenched in Saddam's Cult of Personality," *The China Post*, April 4, 2003. Online at http://www.rickross.com/reference/general/general539.html (as of January 20, 2005).

[63] See Third Infantry Division (Mechanized), *Operation Iraqi Freedom: After Action Report*, Final Draft, Baghdad, Iraq: Headquarters 3rd Infantry Division (Mechanized), May 12, 2003, p. xxii.

[64] Duelfer (2004), p. 62.

[65] Duelfer (2004), p. 66.

[66] Paul Martin, "Iraqi Defense Chief Argued with Saddam," *The Washington Times*, September 21, 2003.

cally sustain a military involvement in which it suffered casualties. He had voiced such a view before the 1991 Gulf War. In his discussion with U.S. Ambassador April Glaspie prior to his invasion of Kuwait, Saddam asserted that America was a "society which cannot accept 10,000 dead in one battle."[67] He later would boast to German television on December 20, 1990—shortly before hostilities commenced—that: "We are sure that if President Bush pushes things toward war, once 5000 of his troops die, he will not be able to continue the war."[68]

Finally, Saddam was apparently unconvinced that the United States really intended to overthrow him.[69] The United States had not marched on Baghdad in 1991, when it had the opportunity to do so after the rout of the Iraqi army in the Kuwait Theater of Operations (KTO).[70] He believed the United States would again see benefits in maintaining his rule and would stop short of a move on Baghdad. The extent of Saddam's persistent illusions about U.S. intentions is summarized in the following statement by the former Director of the Directorate of General Military Intelligence, Staff General Zuhayr Talib 'Abd-al-Satar:

> Two to three months before the war, Saddam Husayn addressed a group of 150 officers. He asked why the Americans would want to come here. Why would the come here when they don't need anything from Iraq? They have already fulfilled the goals that the military established in the first Gulf war. They wanted to occupy the Gulf States and look it has happened. Everyone except for Saddam Husayn, his children, and his inner circle, everyone

---

[67] "Excerpts from Iraqi Transcripts of Meeting with U.S. Envoy," *The New York Times*, September 23, 1990, p. 19.

[68] See *FBIS Trends*, FB TM 91-002, January 10, 1991, p. 2.

[69] Duelfer (2004), p. 32.

[70] According to General Wafic Al Samarrai, the head of Iraqi military intelligence during the Gulf War, Saddam was "quite desperate and frightened" by the prospect of a Coalition march on Baghdad following the rout of his army in the KTO as he believed "his downfall was imminent." When Saddam subsequently learned that President Bush had called for a cease-fire, his morale rose from "zero to 100" (Interview with Lieutenant General Wafic Samarrai, "The Gulf War: An Oral History," *Frontline*, PBS, January 28, 1997. Online at http://www.pbs.org/wgbh/pages/frontline/gulf/oral/samarrai/1.html [as of June 26, 2007]).

else secretly believed that the war would continue all the way to occupation. Saddam and his inner circle thought that the war would last a few days and then it would be over. They thought there would be a few air strikes and maybe some operations in the south.[71]

The Consequences of Saddam's Strategic Misjudgments

Saddam's misjudgments about U.S. intentions vis-à-vis Iraq following 9/11, the likely nature and scope of any U.S. attacks, and Iraq's ability to mount an effective defense with the strategy at hand, importantly influenced Iraq's political and military behavior in the run-up to and conduct of the 2003 war.

First, because he clearly misread the potential peril his regime faced after 9/11, Saddam failed to take the steps that might have helped fend off a U.S. attack. His ill-considered reaction to the terrorist attacks on the United States contributed to Iraq's further international isolation and opprobrium. Saddam missed an opportunity to cast Iraq in a better light when he dismissed suggestions from some of his ministers that he offer to "step forward and have a talk with the Americans," and that in particular, he clarify that Iraq was "not with the terrorists."[72] Prior to November 2002, Saddam made no substantive moves to convince the world that Iraq possessed no weapons of mass destruction. He still refused to accept United Nations Security Council Resolution 1284 or to allow UN weapons inspectors to return to Iraq.[73]

The conviction that the United States would not invade Iraq seems to have led Saddam to be more leisurely than he otherwise might have been in responding to Security Council Resolution 1441, which called on Iraq to "provide UNMOVIC and the IAEA [International Atomic Energy Agency] immediate, unimpeded, unconditional, and unrestricted access to any and all" Iraqi facilities and records they wished

---

[71] Quoted in Duelfer (2004), p. 66.

[72] Duelfer (2004), p. 61.

[73] Duelfer (2004), pp. 61–62.

to inspect and persons they wished to interview.[74] As Hans Blix points out, Iraq's response to Resolution 1441 was a case of too little too late. Blix found it puzzling that the Iraqis did not do more, earlier, to try to convince UNMOVIC that its WMD had been destroyed.[75]

Second, Saddam's erroneous perceptions about the immediacy of the threat also help to explain why Iraq's preparations to fend off an invasion lacked a sense of urgency. Defensive measures were instituted, but as Chapter Four will show, the planning, organization, and implementation of the defense measures appeared to be ad hoc and last-minute.

Third, misjudgments about the Iraqi ability to exact sufficient U.S. casualties to force a political settlement in the event of an invasion led Saddam to eschew adopting the more draconian defensive measures that might have made the invasion more difficult and costly for the Coalition. Because he did not see his regime to be in mortal danger, he apparently did not see the need for scorched-earth tactics, such as blowing up dams to flood likely invasion routes or clouding Iraq's sky and denying Iraq's oil facilities to advancing enemy forces by setting them on fire. Instead, the Iraqi strategy was to try to defend the oil facilities and dams. Saddam's reluctance to allow the systematic demolition of Iraq's bridges is also a manifestation of this complacency. It seems likely that the rationale for disassembling aircraft and hiding them in fields and burying Iraqi jet fighters in the sand was the expectation that they would be needed again following a political settlement.[76]

Finally, erroneous beliefs about U.S. casualty sensitivity and Iraqi military capabilities and morale probably hardened Saddam's determination not to consider defensive options (such as the deployment

---

[74] United Nations Security Council Resolution 1441 on Iraq, adopted on December 20, 2002.

[75] Among the actions Blix found puzzling was the Iraqis being "so late in presenting UNMOVIC with lists of people who they claimed had taken part in the destruction of prohibited items in 1991. . . . Why did they not present these people for interviews in December 2002?" (Blix, 2004, p. 240).

[76] Moore (2003), p. A1.

of Republican Guard heavy divisions in Baghdad) that might have increased the threat of a military coup against his person and regime.

CHAPTER THREE

Saddam's Internal Security Concerns Weakened Iraqi Defenses Against External Attack

Saddam's preoccupation with internal threats also importantly shaped Iraq's defensive posture. Although Saddam believed that much of the Iraqi military and populace would fight to defend Iraq, he trusted neither group as far as his own personal security and that of his regime was concerned. His caution was based on hard experience, as he had been the target of multiple uprisings, coups, and assassination attempts during the course of his rule.

According to the testimony of his associates, Saddam believed he was under the constant threat of an attack and, as a consequence, gave priority to preserving his personal security over all other matters. The widespread Shia and Kurdish uprisings that occurred at the end of the 1991 Gulf War had focused Saddam's attention on the potential threat to his regime from internal rebellion.[1] His paranoia about assassination became particularly acute following the defection to Jordan of his favorite son-in-law, Husein Kamil, in 1995 and the wounding of his son Uday during an assassination attempt in 1996. After the latter attack, Saddam became noticeably less accessible to senior Iraqi officials and increasingly preoccupied with regime security.[2]

---

[1] Woods et al. (2006), pp. 31–32, 51–52.

[2] According to the testimony of former Deputy Prime Minister and Minister of Military Industrialization Huwaysh, the serious wounding of Uday had a particularly deep impact on Saddam because the security procedures and "extensive infrastructure designed to protect him and his family failed in a spectacular and public way" (Duelfer, 2004, p. 21).

Saddam's Personal Security Measures Were Extreme

To foil direct attacks on his person, Saddam adopted a number of extreme security measures. To avoid being targeted for an air attack by the United States, Saddam avoided the use of potential emitters. He reported that he had used a telephone only twice since 1990. He also claimed that he had ordered the building of additional palaces so that the United States would find it more difficult to ascertain his whereabouts.[3] He was clearly aware that the United States had made an energetic effort to kill him during the 1991 Gulf War.[4]

The Iraqi leader's primary defense against attacks on his person was to move frequently, avoid the use of headquarters facilities, conduct business from a variety of ever-changing safe houses in residential areas, and limit the information about his location and planned movements to a very small circle of trusted assistants and bodyguards, virtually all of whom were family or fellow tribal members.[5]

Saddam's meetings with his Cabinet ministers, members of the RCC, and other groups were usually called on short notice and were held in safe houses at undisclosed locations. Attendees were collected by official cars, driven to a pick-up point, and then switched to different vehicles with blacked out windows for the trip between the pick-up point and the meeting place. Attendees were never told where they were once they arrived at the meeting, and were returned home in the same, secure manner as they had been collected.[6] These procedures continued to be followed during OIF.

Because of the tight security surrounding Saddam's whereabouts, Saddam's senior associates were sometimes unable to contact the Iraqi leader for days. Taha Yasin Ramadan Al Jizrawi, one of Saddam's vice

---

[3]   Duelfer (2004), p. 11

[4]   See Stephen T. Hosmer, *Operations Against Enemy Leaders*, Santa Monica, Calif.: RAND Corporation, MR-1385-AF, 2001, pp. 13–15 and 41–43.

[5]   Saddam's personal security was the responsibility of the Presidential bodyguards, Special Security Organization (SSO) security units, and the Special Republican Guard elements. Saddam's food was tested in a laboratory operated by the SSO. See Duelfer (2004), p. 21.

[6]   Duelfer (2004), p. 12.

presidents, reports that it would sometimes "take three days to get in touch with Saddam."[7]

Iraq's Forces Were Shaped to Forestall Coups, Uprisings

The prevention of coups and uprisings was also an overriding concern of Saddam. Distrusting his military commanders and elements of the Iraqi population, the Iraqi leader enacted policies to constrain their motivation and ability to move against him. As a consequence, many of the measures and policies on personnel, organization, command and control, and deployment that shaped and governed Iraq's military and security forces were designed more for forestalling coups and uprisings than for defending the country against foreign invasion.

First, Saddam routinely gave his senior commanders cash bonuses, new cars, Rolex watches and the like to encourage their loyalty and dependence on his largesse. Four days before the war, at the end of the pep-talk meeting Saddam held with 150 of his general officers, for example, Saddam's aides handed each general a cash gift of 1 million dinars, equivalent to about $5,000. At a similar audience two years before, the cash gift to each attendee had been about $20,000.[8] Such gifts were the carrots that accompanied the sticks of threatened imprisonment and execution that Saddam wielded to ensure the loyalty of his senior officers.

Second, Saddam appointed members of his immediate and extended family and members of his Tikriti clan to key military positions and battlefield commands. In doing so, he was quite willing to sacrifice military experience and competency for assured loyalty to his person and regime. Among the most notorious recipients of such appointments were Saddam's sons. Qusay, who had almost no significant military training or service, was entrusted with the "supervision" of the Republican Guard, the Special Republican Guard, and the

---

[7] Duelfer (2004), p. 11.

[8] This according to General Kareem Saadoun, an Air Force commander who attended both meetings. Moore, 2003, p. A1.

SSO. Saddam's other son, Uday, who organized and commanded the Fedayeen Saddam, had equally little training in military matters.

Iraq's commanders at the corps and division levels were more likely to be experienced officers. But, even at this level, command positions were increasingly filled by officers of marginal competence who were members of the Tikriti clan or Saddam's extended family.

Third, to inhibit the leaders of any single military institution from gaining a monopoly of power that might encourage them to challenge his rule, Saddam established a multiplicity of competing military and militia organizations. The most prominent of these were the Fedayeen Saddam and Ba'ath Party militias, which were specifically charged with maintaining population control and suppressing any uprisings, and the Regular Army, Republican Guard, Special Republican Guard, and the Al Quds Army militia.[9] Each of these organizations had a separate chain of command that invariably ended with Saddam. Cooperation among these organizations was officially discouraged and strictly controlled. In addition, some of the organizations actively disliked each other, in part because of the favoritism shown to one over another.

Fourth, Saddam embedded intelligence and Ba'ath Party personnel within Iraqi military organizations to monitor officers and troops. Ba'athist political officers were emplaced in the senior echelons of Iraqi divisions to ensure loyalty and compliance with Baghdad's orders. Officers of the Directorate of General Military Intelligence were assigned to each military unit down to battalion level to monitor troops and control corruption. The SSO embedded security officers down to battalion level within Republican Guard units. The mission of these SSO officers was to monitor the military commanders to guarantee their political reliability and loyalty. The Ba'ath Party and intelligence officers

---

[9]   The Al Quds Army was a civilian militia organized by Saddam in 2001 "in theory to prepare for an invasion of Israel" (Al Quds is the Arabic name for Jerusalem). But as war with the United States became imminent, homeland defense became its primary role. The Iraqi government claimed the militia has 7 million members, but Western analysts put the number at closer to 1 million. The militia members received little training and were lightly armed. See Rajiv Chandrasekaran, "Iraq Arms Civilians as Second Line of Defense Against U.S.," *The Washington Post*, February 5, 2003, p. A1.

reported through their own chains of command to Saddam.[10] Among other monitoring methods, the SSO officers routinely maintained taps on commander's phones and in their offices, homes, and automobiles. Pseudo coup groups were also established by the security organizations to entrap in sting operations those who might be disloyal.

Fifth, Saddam and his headquarters' staffs kept an extremely close eye and tight rein on the actions of the Iraqi corps, division, and subordinate commanders. To discourage untoward collusion between military units, commanders were forbidden, without explicit authorization, to interact with neighboring units not under their direct chain of command. In addition, Republican Guard and Regular Army units and equipment could not be moved without explicit prior permission from Baghdad.[11] These restrictions carried over even into combat. Special Republican Guard troops, whose primary mission was the physical protection and security of the presidential palaces, grounds, and other sites sensitive to national security, were not permitted to enter any presidential grounds without the prior approval of Saddam.[12]

Sixth, to forestall coups, no Regular Army or Republican Guard units were deployed in or allowed to enter Baghdad.

Finally, to deter and uncover potential uprisings, Saddam's security operatives and Ba'ath Party officials maintained extensive informant nets within the Iraqi population centers to monitor possible antiregime behavior. In the event of uprisings in Baghdad, security was to be restored by Saddam Fedayeen and Ba'athist militias, local police forces, and SSO elements.[13] To prevent the infiltration of insurgent elements from Iran, Saddam positioned Iraqi forces along the Iraqi-Iranian border.

---

[10] See Duelfer (2004), pp. 83 and 89.

[11] In the case of the Republican Guard, some of whose forces were closest to Baghdad, "no piece of military equipment could be moved—even for repair—by brigade, division, or corps commander without the prior written permission of Qusay through the RG Secretariat" (Duelfer, 2004, p. 93).

[12] Duelfer (2004), p. 93.

[13] A battalion-sized SSO unit was responsible for the security of strategically important roads around Baghdad and Tikrit. Duelfer, 2004, p. 92.

The Consequences of Saddam's Fixation on Internal Security

The measures Saddam instituted to ensure his personal security and to fortify his regime against coups and uprisings had several consequences.

First, Saddam's personal security measures made a successful decapitation strike against him problematic. The two attempts to strike Saddam during OIF failed because of a lack of accurate, up-to-the-minute information on his whereabouts. Saddam was not at the Dora Farm when it was struck on March 19, but his daughter Raghad (who owned the farm) was present and barely missed being killed.[14] The next attempt may have come closer. According to some sources, who may not have had first-hand knowledge of the event, Saddam had been at a safe house behind a restaurant in Baghdad's Mansour district shortly before it was struck on April 7, but he had left almost immediately because he suspected treachery and expected an air strike on that locale.[15] Another account holds that Saddam never actually visited the safe house, but also suggests that he planted information about his planned presence there to invite an air attack and thereby expose disloyal Iraqis in his entourage.[16]

---

[14] Raghad reported that she had left her house at Dora Farm several hours before the strike and had moved into a "a very simple military shelter" on the farm with her two children. She reports that "even the smallest buildings" on the farm were destroyed. See "Al-Arabiyah TV Interviews Saddam's Daughter Raghad," Dubai Al-Arabiyah Television in Arabic, August 1, 2003. FBIS Document ID: GMP200308011000231. Online at https://portal.rccb.osis.gov/servlet/Repository?encoded=xml_products:GMP20030801000231 (as of August 24, 2003).

[15] According to Uday Hussein's personal bodyguard, Saddam became suspicious that there was an informant in his camp after several of his safe houses had come under attack. Saddam asked the officer he suspected, a captain, to prepare a meeting at a safe house behind a restaurant as a test. Saddam and his entourage arrived at the safe house and left almost immediately. "Ten minutes after they went out of the door, it was bombed" according to the bodyguard. Saddam had the captain summarily executed. See Catherine Philp, "Secrets of Saddam's Family at War," *Timesonline*, June 25, 2003. A slightly different account of why Saddam immediately abandoned the April 7 meeting in the Mansour district is provided by a former senior Iraqi government minister in "Treachery: How Iraq Went to War Against Saddam," *London Sunday Times*, January 11, 2004.

[16] See Gordon and Trainor (2006a), p. 409.

Second, the U.S. hopes that the "shock and awe" created by the bombing of dozens of key targets simultaneously would cause Saddam's regime to "crumble" would go unrealized.[17] There was an expectation that kinetic bombing would be "especially effective" against Iraqi leadership ("the real inner circle of Saddam and his two sons, Uday and Qusay"), and the Iraqi internal security services ("including the close-in ring of bodyguards in the Special Security Organization"), and the command, control, and communications network.[18] Implicit in the selection of these target sets was the assumption that their destruction would either eliminate the regime's key leaders; destroy the regime's ability to command and control Iraq's military forces; or strip Saddam of his security protection to the point where he would become vulnerable to assassination or overthrow by a coup or uprising.

The chances of a Shia uprising during OIF were minimal, given the devastation the Shias had suffered following their abortive uprising against Saddam at the end of the Gulf War. The United States had publicly encouraged the Iraqis to rise up but refused to provide any support once the uprising was under way.[19] Tens of thousands of Shia were killed during Saddam's retaliatory operations. As a consequence, Shias were loath to go down this risky path once again in OIF. And as has been discussed above, Saddam had organized, structured, and deployed his security, military, and militia forces to prevent coups and suppress possible uprisings.

Moreover, Saddam and his colleagues expected such air attacks and prepared for them by avoiding facilities likely to be targeted. The air campaigns in Desert Storm and Desert Fox had sensitized Iraqi military and civilian leaders to the types of targets the United States

---

[17] Secretary of Defense Donald Rumsfeld expressed interest in designing a bombing campaign that would "put very rapid, very quick pressure early on" that might cause Saddam's regime to crumble. See Bob Woodward, *Plan of Attack*, New York: Simon and Schuster, 2004, pp. 75 and 76, 110, 410. Also see Gordon and Trainor (2006a), p. 82.

[18] These were the top items on Central Command (CENTCOM) Commander General Tommy Frank's list of the centers of gravity in Saddam's government. See Woodward (2004), pp. 56–57. Also see Gordon and Trainor (2006a), p. 210.

[19] Many of the dissident Shia leaders apparently expected such U.S. support. See Hosmer (2001), pp. 71–75.

was likely to attack, and these facilities were typically evacuated before hostilities began. By early March, numerous senior Iraqi officers and officials in Baghdad had already moved to government-owned safe houses or to newly rented civilian houses.[20] As a consequence, the 50 attacks on time-sensitive leadership targets during OIF produced zero kills of the targeted personages.[21] Indeed, none of the 200 top officials in the regime was killed by air strikes.[22]

Third, the measures Saddam adopted to ensure his personal security almost certainly degraded his situational awareness and ability to command and control Iraqi forces in a timely manner. Saddam's avoidance of the use of the telephone and headquarters facilities, his constant movement and use of residential safe houses, and his sometime inaccessibility to subordinates undoubtedly made it more difficult for him to see the battlefield and probably delayed the authorization of military actions, such as the blowing up of bridges, that required his consent.[23]

Finally, Saddam's preoccupation with internal threats undoubtedly weakened Iraqi capabilities to counter a conventional invasion such as occurred in OIF. As Chapter Four will show, actions to fortify his regime against coups and uprisings compromised the adoption of an effective Iraqi defensive strategy, degraded the quality of military

---

[20] Some of the newly rented facilities lacked telephones or radio communications, and, as a result, orders had to be conveyed in writing and delivered by car or motorcycle. Colonel Rafed Abdul Mehdi, who organized the deployment of antiaircraft missiles from a house in east Baghdad, reported that he sometimes received as many as 20 written orders a day from his commander. More-junior officers, such as helicopter pilots, also moved to safe houses in Baghdad. See Vivienne Walt, "Chaos Ruled Before Iraq's Military Fell," *Boston Globe*, August 25, 2003. Online at http://www.hench.net/2003/z082503a.htm (as of June 14, 2007).

[21] See statement by Marc Garlasco, a DIA analyst from 1997 to 2003, in Frontline Transcript (2004).

[22] Gordon and Trainor (2006a), p. 177.

[23] Saddam was known to use over a dozen safe houses in Baghdad. See Michael R. Gordon and Bernard E. Trainor, "Iraqi Leader, in Frantic Flight, Eluded U.S. Strikes," *The New York Times*, March 12, 2006b, p. 6.

leadership and decisionmaking, and undermined the coordination and unity of command of the Iraqi forces resisting the Coalition advance.

CHAPTER FOUR

Iraq's Military Strategy and Operations Were Poorly Designed and Executed

Saddam's strategic miscalculations and the policies and practices that flowed from his preoccupation with internal threats significantly degraded the Iraqi defense in OIF. Indeed, the Iraqi leader's perceptions, decisions, and practices explain in large measure why the Iraqi resistance against OIF was so poorly planned and led. The pernicious effects of these shortcomings were compounded by the fact that Iraqi units were poorly positioned on the battlefield, lacked situational awareness, were inadequately trained, and were equipped with weaponry that was decidedly inferior to that of the Coalition.

Saddam's Military Strategy Was Flawed

As noted in preceding chapters, Saddam believed that the United States would limit its military attacks on Iraq to bombing and would not invade the country because of the casualties an invasion would entail. However, in the event of an invasion, the overall Iraqi political-military strategy was to protract the conflict, maximize U.S. casualties, and publicize the humanitarian costs of the conflict, thereby creating U.S. domestic and international pressures for a negotiated solution that would allow Saddam's regime to remain in place.[1]

The defensive scheme Saddam adopted to execute this overall strategy focused on the defense of Baghdad and other major Iraqi

---

[1] See Duelfer (2003), p. 68.

cities. As reflected by Iraqi force deployments, the strategy called for (1) Regular Army forces to defend forward, impede any Coalition advance into the country, and protect the major cities in northern and southern Iraq, (2) Republican Guard forces (eventually reinforced by some Regular Army units) to defend the approaches to Baghdad, and (3) paramilitary forces to suppress any anti-regime uprisings and counter any enemy incursions in Baghdad or other cities.

Regular Army Units Largely Remained in Prewar Deployment Areas

Even on the eve of conflict, most of Iraq's Regular Army divisions remained in the vicinity of their prewar deployment areas. In northern Iraq, some 10 Regular Army mechanized and infantry divisions remained facing the Green Line, the de facto border within Iraq separating Kurdish-controlled territory from Iraqi government-controlled territory.[2] These units were responsible for countering any enemy attacks from the north and northeast and for protecting the important cities of Mosul and Kirkuk. Some of these northern units were later moved to central Iraq to assist with the defense of Baghdad.

Six Regular Army armored, mechanized, and infantry divisions were deployed to defend southern Iraq.[3] As the subsequent discussion will show, the positioning of this force was heavily weighted to the east, paralleling the Iraqi-Iranian border. One division, the 51st Mechanized, was positioned south of Basra for the defense of that city, and

---

[2] The units defending along the Green Line were the 1st and 5th Mechanized Divisions and the 2nd, 4th, 7th, 8th, 15th, 16th, 34th, and 38th Infantry Divisions. The 3rd Armored and 34th Infantry Divisions were situated below the southern end of the Green Line, along the border with Iran. The Republican Guard Adnan Mechanized and the Nebuchadnezzar Infantry Divisions, which normally had been positioned in the north, were moved down to the Baghdad area to strengthen the defense of the capital. Other Iraqi divisions were also moved south during the course of the war. See Fontenot, Degen, and Tohn (2004), pp. 100, 212, 248, 252, 263, 296, 301, and 330, and CFLCC Intelligence Update, March 23, 2003, 0300Z.

[3] The units defending southern Iraq were the 6th and 10th Armored Divisions, the 51st Mechanized Division, and the 11th, 14th, and 18th Infantry Divisions. See Fontenot, Degen, and Tohn (2004), pp. 100–101, and CFLCC Intelligence Update, March 23, 2003, 0300Z.

the 11th Infantry Division was positioned to defend the approaches to the cities of An Nasiriyah and As Samawah.

The Republican Guard Was Deployed Outside Baghdad

As the seat of power, Baghdad was accorded Iraq's strongest defenses. Saddam deployed his six Republican Guard divisions (three armored, one mechanized, and two infantry) in a cordon around Baghdad, with particular emphasis on defending the southern approaches to the city.[4] Regular Army infantry units were later also positioned in the Baghdad area to supplement these Republican Guard forces.

Saddam's plan for the defense of Baghdad called for the preparation of four concentric defensive rings around the capital. Reconnaissance elements were to be deployed in the outermost ring, and Republican Guard and Special Republican Guard forces were to be situated initially in the third defensive circle. If hard-pressed by attacking U.S. units, the Republican Guard forces were, upon Saddam's order, to retreat in concert to the second inner defensive ring. If forced back into the final (innermost) "Red" defensive belt, the remaining Iraqi units were expected to "fight to the death."[5]

Saddam's expectation was that the combined Republican Guard and Regular Army divisions forming the perimeter around Baghdad would be able to fend off any U.S. forces that attempted to approach the capital along the major lines of communication. Saddam was prepared for the possibility that Baghdad might be subjected to a prolonged siege, but he apparently never contemplated that the capital might actually be lost.[6]

Some Iraqi Republican Guard commanders had serious reservations about Saddam's defensive scheme when the ring plan was briefed to them on December 18, 2002. Among other shortcomings, the plan

---

[4] The Republican Guard forces were the Al-Nida, Hammurabi, and Medina Armored Divisions, the Adnan Mechanized Division, and the Baghdad and Nebuchadnezzar Infantry Divisions.

[5] Details of the plan were provided by Lieutenant General Hamdani, the Republican Guard II Corps Commander. See Woods et al. (2006), pp. 80–81.

[6] See Duelfer (2004), p. 62.

failed to take sufficient account of the varied terrain around Baghdad or the serious difficulties Iraqi forces would face if they attempted to conduct simultaneous retreats from one ring to another when engaged by U.S. ground and air forces. But when Republican Guard commanders gently voiced concerns about the plan, they were told that no changes were permitted because Saddam had already signed the plan.[7]

According to Iraqi sources, little further defensive planning or discussion occurred after the December 18 meeting. Some senior commanders, including the Commander of Republican Guard forces in II Corps, remained uncertain about elements of the actual defensive plan to be employed beyond the orders they may have received about disposition of forces in their own immediate areas of responsibility.[8] Coordination between division and corps commanders was lacking because of Saddam's previously mentioned policy prohibiting battlefield commanders from meeting or otherwise interacting with commanders outside their own chain of command, including the commanders of immediate neighboring units. In the end, the four-ring plan as originally approved by Saddam was never executed as planned, although Republican Guard and Regular Army forces were positioned around Baghdad in some variant of a defensive belt and were, at the last moment, ordered to pull back into Baghdad.[9]

---

[7] Woods et al. (2006), pp. 80–81.

[8] One senior Iraqi officer believed that there were two defensive belts. The brigadier general who commanded Baghdad's missile air defense told an interviewer that "the defense of Baghdad was planned with two belts of army defenders, one set 100 kilometers from the city, the other at 50 kilometers" (Robert Fisk, "Ruling the Airways—How America Demoralized Iraq's Army," *The Independent (UK)*, May 24, 2003. Online at http://web.lexis-nexis.com/ universe/document?_m=d94acd59d2a42e30ab941b70369be73 [as of June 10, 2004]).

[9] Lieutenant Colonel Tariq Mohammed of the Republican Guard Medina Division reported: "We had four concentric circles of defense. But when the U.S. moved up through the desert, we were to go back into the cities. The huge mistake was moving the Republican Guard all the time. The soldiers were exhausted." Mohammed stated that by early April, most of the division's soldiers had drifted off. On April 6, Mohammed got into his car and drove to Baghdad. See Walt (2003).

Militia Forces Were Positioned Inside Cities

Under Saddam's defensive scheme, the task of engaging any enemy troops that might penetrate into the cities was to fall primarily on Iraqi paramilitary forces. These militia units were, from Saddam's standpoint, to perform the even-more-important mission of deterring, and if need be, suppressing any anti-regime uprisings in the urban areas.[10]

Saddam probably envisioned at least three contingencies that could give rise to threatening popular uprisings:

- an attack limited only to bombing, during the course of which the Coalition or Iran would attempt to foment a Shi'ite or other antigovernment uprisings. Saddam was continually worried about possible Iranian political machinations in Iraq.[11]
- an invasion in which the Coalition, in order to hold down casualties, stopped short of attempting to overrun the entire country, and instead seized Basra and other southern towns for use as bargaining chips and positions from which to provoke and support anti-regime uprisings[12]
- an invasion in which one or more Iraqi cities were forced to hold out against a prolonged siege, situations in which public uprisings would have to be rapidly quelled lest the defense collapse.

To ensure public order and provide for the internal defense of Baghdad, Saddam organized and positioned thousands of Fedayeen Saddam and Ba'ath Party militiamen inside the city. Three Special Republican Guard brigades were also positioned in Baghdad, both to

---

[10] According to an analysis of Iraqi prisoner interrogations compiled by the U.S. Joint Forces Command, Saddam was so convinced that war could be averted or that the United States would attack Iraq with only a limited bombing campaign that he deployed Iraqi forces to crush possible domestic uprisings rather than to defend against external attacks. See Woods et al. (2006), pp. 29–32. Also see Third Infantry Division (2003), pp. xxii–xxiii.

[11] See Duelfer (2004), pp. 29, and 31.

[12] Some Iraqi senior officers also believed that the United States would occupy only a portion of Iraq. A variant of this enclave strategy had been suggested by Paul Wolfowitz and others during the 1990s as a means of bringing about regime change in Iraq. See Duelfer (2004), p. 67, and Stephen J. Solarz and Paul Wolfowitz, "How to Overthrow Saddam," Letters to the Editor, *Foreign Affairs*, March/April 1999, p. 160.

counter any incursions or uprisings and to provide area security for Saddam and protect his palaces.[13]

Saddam also established a large Fedayeen Saddam and Ba'ath Party militia presence within the southern cities (including Basra, Umm Qasr, Nasiriyah, As Samawah, An Najaf, and Al Hillah).[14] He also positioned some Fedayeen Saddam units along with a robust Ba'ath Party militia presence in the northern cities of Mosul and Kirkuk. Al Quds militiamen and recently armed tribal elements were also counted on to contribute to the internal defense of some cities.

Saddam took two other actions to deter possible popular uprisings. First, he directed his intelligence services and Ba'athist leaders to closely monitor the populations in their local areas. Second, he directed that the principal urban areas be provided with sufficient supplies of food to withstand protracted bombing or sieges by ground forces.

To generate international and U.S. domestic pressures to halt the invasion, Fedayeen Saddam elements were reportedly directed to use intimidation and threats to force local civilian elements in the cities to fight the invading Coalition troops, thereby creating Coalition-caused civilian casualties. Iraqi combatants were apparently also directed to draw Coalition forces into causing collateral damage by deploying units and equipment in or near mosques, schools, historical sites, and heavily populated civilian housing areas.[15] However, Iraqi commanders probably also hoped that the positioning of their forces inside or next to such facilities would provide them with sanctuary from air and ground attack.

---

[13] The Special Republican Guard, which probably numbered about 15,000 troops, were among the few Iraqi forces that had received some training in urban warfare. (Fontenot, Degen, and Tohn, 2004, p. 99.)

[14] See Third Infantry Division (2003), p. xxii.

[15] The Third Infantry Division frequently observed such Iraqi behavior, which supports the inference that the Iraqi forces were directed to act as they did. See Third Infantry Division (2003), pp. xxii–xxiii.

Saddam's Military Strategy Had Shortcomings and Vulnerabilities

The military strategy that Saddam adopted to meet the Coalition invasion did little to provide effective support to his overarching political-military objectives of protracting the conflict, maximizing U.S. casualties, and, thereby, creating pressures for a negotiated solution that would leave his regime in place. Indeed, the defensive scheme he adopted hastened the Iraqi defeat and failed to exploit potential options for protracting the conflict and maximizing Coalition casualties.

The flaws in the Iraqi military strategy appear to be attributable to Saddam's congenital optimism, lack of military acumen, and failure to absorb the lessons of Desert Storm; misjudgments about Coalition intentions, vulnerabilities, and likely courses of action; misperceptions about the military capabilities and fighting will of his own forces; and overriding concern to fend off internal threats to his person and regime. The strategy was also the product of Iraq's dated military doctrine and the climate of fear that deterred any disagreement with Saddam's decisions from the cowed general officers and senior officials that populated the higher echelons of the Iraqi defense establishment.

Iraqi Forces in the South Were Poorly Positioned. Most of the Iraqi divisions in southern Iraq were not positioned well to meet an invasion from Kuwait. Even after OIF was under way, the bulk of the Regular Army divisions in southern Iraq (including the 10th and 6th Armored Divisions, 51st Mechanized Division, and the 14th and 18th Infantry Divisions) remained positioned to defend the Highway 6 (Tigris River) approach toward Baghdad.[16] Highway 6 was only one of several routes of march to the capital; it was by no means the most likely to be chosen by the Coalition. The orientation along Route 6 also maintained these forces near their normal deployment areas paralleling the Iraq-Iran border and probably reflected Saddam's concern that Iran might attempt to militarily exploit a Coalition air or ground attack. Saddam saw Iran as "Iraq's abiding enemy" and was "keenly aware that, in addition to the potential of invasion, Iranian infiltrators could cause internal unrest." Saddam believed that "Iran was the main

---

[16] Fontenot, Degen, and Tohn (2004), pp. 99–101. Also see CFLCC Intelligence Update, March 23, 2003, 0300Z.

concern because it wanted to annex southern Iraq" and that "U.S. air strikes were less of a worry than an Iranian land attack."[17]

Whatever the reason, the continued deployment of the Regular Army armored and infantry divisions along the Highway 6 corridor near the Iranian border left the door open for Coalition advances further west along Highways 7 and 8, the western Euphrates River approach to Baghdad, which had far fewer forces defending them. These forces were limited to a brigade of the 18th Infantry Division that was positioned to defend the Rumaila oil field, a Regular Army mechanized infantry brigade, and elements of two Regular Army armored brigades. The Regular Army's 11th Infantry Division also defended farther north along the approaches to Nasiriyah.[18]

The unbalanced force dispositions in southern Iraq were undoubtedly part of the reason Coalition commanders concluded that "Saddam had not positioned his forces to counter a ground assault."[19] As one history of the war put it: "When the Coalition's invasion began, Iraqi forces were in none of the places they should have been to be militarily effective."[20]

The Concentration of Forces Outside Cities Exposed Them to Coalition Attack. An important consequence of a military strategy that directed Republican Guard and Regular Army divisions to defend outside Iraqi cities was that it made those divisions extremely vulnerable to piecemeal destruction by U.S. air and ground forces. Indeed, the placement of Iraqi forces exterior to Baghdad was far more to the liking of U.S. commanders than was the prospect of an urban fight in a "Fortress Baghdad," which President Bush and other U.S. leaders feared could prove both time-consuming and costly in American lives.[21]

---

[17] Iraqi ground forces had remained oriented toward the Iranian border after Desert Storm. See Duelfer (2004), p. 29.

[18] See Fontenot, Degen, and Tohn (2004), pp. 99–101.

[19] See Woodward (2004), p. 402.

[20] See Williamson Murray and Robert H. Scales, Jr., *The Iraq War*, Cambridge, Mass.: Harvard University Press, 2003, p. 96.

[21] The CENTCOM Commander, General Tommy Franks, had developed an "Inside-Out" concept for preventing outlying Iraqi Regular Army or Republican Guard divisions from

Some senior Iraqi generals voiced deep concerns about the surviv-ability of any forces concentrated outside the cities. Lieutenant Gen-eral Raad Al-Hamdani, the II Corps Republican Guard commander responsible for defending the southern approaches to Baghdad, wor-ried greatly about the likely effects of American airpower, even though his Republican Guard divisions had prepared thousands of alternative fighting positions to reduce their vulnerability to air attack.[22]

Other Iraqi officers also disagreed with Saddam's deployment scheme. Major Saleh Abdullah Mahdi Jaburi, a 2nd Infantry Divi-sion battalion commander, said that the decision to deploy Republican Guard forces south of Baghdad at Karabala, Hillah, and Al Kut made them easy targets for Coalition strike aircraft. According to Major Jaburi, the Republican Guard units were particularly vulnerable to American air attack while they were moving, and cost them "a lot of men." In Major Jaburi's view, "It was very easy for the Americans to enter Baghdad."[23]

---

coming back into Baghdad:

> Instead of attacking from the outside of the defensive cordon around the capital, we
> would destroy the enemy inside the cordon by relentless air attack, working from the
> center outward. The more concentrated the Republican Guard positions were, the
> more vulnerable they became. And attacking in and around Baghdad had the added
> benefit of making the city 'inhospitable' to forces looking for a place to hide (Tommy
> Franks, *American Soldier*, New York: HarperCollins Publishers, Inc., 2004, p. 391, and
> Woodward, 2004, pp. 126, 135–136, 147, 206, and 208).

[22] General Hamdani's preferred strategy was to deploy Iraqi forces in small increments far away from the cities and to declare Baghdad an open city to prevent its destruction. How this strategy would have preserved Saddam's regime is unclear. According to Hamdani,

> Even if the enemy entered [Baghdad], that would not mean anything. There should be
> no headquarters in it, and no major state administration organization, so that the enemy
> would be compelled to look for his opponents in all directions. The war would become
> unclear, and the enemy would not be able to say that he had attained his objectives. This
> is because he had to attain his objective on the scale of Iraq, which is a relatively large
> country, by Middle East standards (Interview with Lieutenant General Raad Al-Ham-
> dani, "The Invasion of Iraq: An Oral History," *Frontline*, PBS, posted March 9, 2004.
> Online at http://www.pbs.org/wgbh/pages/frontline/shows/invasion/interviews/raad.
> html [as of February 27, 2004]).

[23] Scott Peterson and Peter Ford, "From Iraqi Officers, Three Tales of Shock and Defeat," *The Christian Science Monitor*, April 18, 2003, pp. 1 and 12.

The Failure to Exploit the Potential of Urban Warfare. The Allied experience in fighting German and Japanese forces in urban areas during World War II, and the U.S. experience in the fights to regain control of Seoul during the Korean War and Hue during the Vietnam War, underscore how time-consuming and costly in casualties urban warfare can be. However, Saddam's military strategy excluded measures that could have made Baghdad and other Iraqi built-up areas more difficult and costly to subdue.

The decision to fight Republican Guard and Regular Army units outside the cities obviously reduced their potential for mounting a later defense within urban areas. Saddam apparently did not believe such a step was necessary. He naively assumed that Iraq's lightly armed Fedayeen and Ba'ath Party militia forces, along with the local Al Quds Army militia and the numerous tribal elements that he had armed shortly before the war, would be able to mount an effective, high-casualty-producing resistance against any Coalition forces that penetrated the urban areas.

Urban warfare was simply not part of Iraqi military doctrine, and none of the Regular Army forces and very few Republican Guard units received any training for city fighting.[24] According to Stephen Biddle, the Regular Army and Republican Guard commanders his team interviewed found the entire concept of city fighting unthinkable. Biddle quoted one Iraqi colonel as saying: "Why would anyone want to fight in a city? Troops couldn't defend themselves in cities."[25]

---

[24] The Republican Guard Al-Nida Armored Division was an exception, having received some training in urban warfare. See Woods et al., 2006, p. 70, n. 82. As previously noted, members of the Special Republican Guards also were given some training in urban warfare. See above, p. 40, n. 13.

[25] See "Prepared Testimony of Dr. Stephen Biddle, Associate Professor of National Security Studies, U.S. Army War College Strategic Studies Institute," before the House Armed Services Committee, October 21, 2003. Online at http://www.globalsecurity.org/military/library/congress/2003_hr/03-10-21biddle.htm (as of June 26, 2007). Dr. Biddle and his team conducted a study of OIF and its implications for American defense policy for the War College. The study was based on a series of 176 interviews with U.S., British, and Iraqi Regular Army and Republican Guard participants in the conflict, primary source materials relating to the conduct of the war, and direct physical inspection of some of the war's key battlefields. See Biddle testimony (2003), footnote 1.

Saddam's concern to keep potentially coup-prone military units at a distance from his seat of power—which was a major barrier to the deployment of Republican Guard and Regular Army divisions inside Baghdad—was undoubtedly a key reason that he purportedly rejected a plan attributed to his Defense Minister, Staff General Sultan Hashim Ahmad Al Ta'i, to "put up 'a powerful defense' through urban warfare in and around Baghdad." General Al Ta'i would have surrounded Baghdad with huge numbers of land mines and ringed the city with T-72 tanks.[26]

As it was, the interior defense of the cities was largely left to lightly armed Fedayeen Saddam and Ba'ath Party militia units, foreign jihadists, and, in the case of Baghdad, also to elements of a single Special Republican Guard infantry division that possessed but a fraction of tanks and other heavy weapons available in Iraq's heavy divisions. Only when the Iraqi battlefield situation became desperate, in early April, were remnants of Regular Army and Republican Guard units brought into the capital.

Effective defense within the cities was further hampered by the near absence of fixed defenses or barricades that would have created strong fighting positions from which Iraqi defenders could have impeded the advance of Coalition armor and infantry. A survey of Iraqi defenses in Baghdad found no defensive preparations, such as barricades, wall reinforcement, loophole construction to permit firing through walls, or wire entanglements, in the interiors of buildings and few, if any, obstacles, minefields, and barriers on the streets. What prepared fighting positions existed were typically outdoors and exposed. The protection surrounding such positions was often one sandbag deep. As a consequence, the militias and Special Republican Guard units often fought in the open or from easily penetrated defensive positions.[27]

---

[26] As described by an unidentified general officer, General Al Ta'i's plan was to defend Iraq by forcing invading forces to engage in urban combat. His battle plan would have included the deployment of troops in small groups of fighters and drawing out the battle, which would have aimed to make the Coalition's advance on the capital slow and painful. General Al Ta'i believed that "neither Bush nor Blair could handle the political pressure at home if [many] soldiers were dead" (Martin, 2003).

[27] Biddle testimony (2003). However, some enemy militia units used cover and proved adept at using "guile, deception, and ambush" (Gordon and Trainor, 2006a, p. 259).

The Failure to Mine Roads, Drop Bridges, Flood Approach Avenues, Deny Use of Port Facilities, and Ignite Oil Fields. Even though the Iraqi strategy was to impede the U.S. march toward Baghdad, measures that could have slowed the American advance, such as the systematic mining of roads, destruction of bridges, and flooding of choke points, were not part of the Iraqi defense scheme.

Former Iraqi military leaders, including a number of detained generals who were interviewed about Iraq's lack of defensive measures, attributed Saddam's failure to prepare land mines and other basic military measures to block or to slow the U.S. advance to the Iraqi president's military incompetence, unfounded optimism, isolation, and overreliance on family and tribe in a time of military crisis.[28]

Permission to drop bridges could be granted only by Baghdad headquarters, and Saddam, misperceiving the military situation, failed to order their systematic demolition. Former Iraqi commanders report that Saddam was so convinced that the Republican Guard units deployed south of Baghdad would be able to repel U.S. armor attacks that he decided not to mine the highways or blow up the bridges leading to the capital: "The infrastructure was left intact so that it could be used by Iraqi forces mounting counterattacks."[29] Saddam apparently also wanted bridges left intact to enable his security and militia forces to promptly move against any anti-regime uprisings.[30]

As a consequence, nearly all the key bridges along the lines of the Coalition's advance and the bridges and causeways within or leading into Baghdad, Basra, and other urban centers were captured intact.[31]

---

[28] See Coll (2003), p. A1.

[29] David Zucchino, "Iraq's Swift Defeat Blamed on Leaders," *Los Angeles Times*, August 11, 2003, p. 1.

[30] See Woods et al. (2006), p. 31.

[31] Thomas Ricks of *The Washington Post* recalls people at the Pentagon telling him about the Iraqi military before the war:

> Sure, their infantry kind of stinks, and their tanks are old. But they've got good engineers, and they're going to blow the bridges. Very few bridges across those rivers were actually blown. Actually, there were a lot of smaller bridges across canals, because that area between the rivers is just chock-a-block with canals. It could have been a real nightmare for the U.S. military, even if just the engineers had been out blow-

Some were prepared for demolition but not blown; others were not even wired.[32]

Sometimes the authorization to destroy a bridge came too late. The Republican Guard II Corps Commander, General Hamdani, reports that he gave the commander of the Republican Guard bridge-demolition unit at the al-Kaed Bridge (Objective Peach) on the Euphrates River southwest of Baghdad "clear written and verbal orders" to blow the bridge whenever he felt the Americans were getting close. But General Hamdani's orders were not carried out because the on-the-spot Iraqi commander awaited authorization from Baghdad and the order to destroy the bridge "was not issued in time."[33]

If Saddam saw no need for the systematic mining of roads or destruction of bridges, he was obviously unwilling to entertain the even more drastic option of breaching dams and dikes to flood the lower Tigris and Euphrates River Valleys and the other potential choke points along the U.S. line of march. American commanders worried about such contingencies and were particularly concerned that the Iraqis might blow the Hadithah Dam, which contained the waters of a huge reservoir immediately north of the Karbala Gap. Had the dam been breached, the resulting flood would have made an armored movement through the gap impossible.[34] American Ranger elements secured the dam on April 1 and had to fend off counterattacks from Iraqi forces for about a week. However, there is no evidence that the Iraqis ever intended to breach the Hadithah Dam, as they had ample opportunity

---

ing up bridges, mining choke points between the canals. And not a lot of that happened (Interview with Thomas E. Ricks, "The Invasion of Iraq: An Oral History," *Frontline*, PBS, posted March 9, 2004. Online at http://www.pbs.org/wgbh/pages/frontline/shows/invasion/interviews/ricks.html [as of February 27, 2004]).

[32] The Iraqis made no systematic effort to destroy the militarily important bridges at Nasiriyah. Similarly, none of the five bridges surrounding Basra was destroyed, although one was wired for demolition. Biddle testimony (2003). The charges under one bridge were detonated, but the bridge failed to collapse. See Murray and Scales (2003), pp. 205–206.

[33] Interview with Lieutenant General Hamdani (2004).

[34] The gap to the west of Karbala was the only feasible route of advance as the area to the east of Karbala and around the Euphrates River crossing was a "nightmare of bogs and obstacles" (Murray and Scales, 2003, pp. 203–204).

to do so before the Rangers seized it. Indeed, the Iraqis attempted no major flooding. According to Biddle, the closest they "came to deliberate flooding was some small-scale tactical inundation in the Subiyat Depression near An Nasiriyah."[35]

Saddam's confidence that his military strategy would force a negotiated settlement that would leave his regime in place apparently also dissuaded him from ordering the destruction of the port of Umm Qasr and the torching of Iraq's oil facilities.

The Coalition did not plan to rely on the Iraqi port of Umm Qasr for the logistics support of their invasion forces; however, the Iraqis did not know that. They had an option to block and delay the Coalition's use of the port by sinking ships in its harbor and destroying its handling facilities. Even though the Iraqis held the port for days after the outbreak of hostilities, Coalition forces captured the port intact.[36]

Coalition planners worried that Saddam would react to an invasion by systematically torching the country's oil wells and destroying its production facilities. The concern was so great that forces were inserted into Iraq's southern Rumaila oil field at the outset of the conflict to prevent such destruction. A possible Iraqi motivation for torching the southern Rumaila fields and the northern Kirkuk fields would have been to create a vast overcast of smoke to obscure and contaminate the Iraqi battlefield. The Iraqis routinely set oil trenches afire around Baghdad in an attempt to make air attacks on the city more difficult. Also, Saddam might have ordered the torching of the fields as a scorched-earth tactic that would present the invading Coalition forces with an environmental nightmare and economic disaster, putting international pressure on Washington to end the fighting.

As it was, Saddam apparently saw no reason to destroy Iraq's precious petroleum infrastructure. There is no evidence that the Iraqi leader made preparations for any systematic destruction of Iraq's oil fields. The very limited demolitions that occurred in Rumaila fields (nine wells out of 250) were probably an attempt to deter the Coalition invasion from going forward. None of the pumping stations, gas-oil

---

[35] See Biddle testimony (2003).

[36] See Biddle testimony (2003).

separation plants, or pipelines at Rumaila were prepared for demolition.[37] If these facilities and the remainder of the wells at Rumaila had been wired for detonation, the Iraqis would have had adequate time to destroy the field before it was secured by Coalition forces. Iraqi forces maintained control of the Kirkuk fields in northern Iraq for more than three weeks after the invasion began, yet none of the Kirkuk wells and other oil facilities in the area was destroyed or even prepared for demolition.[38]

The Failure to Attack Coalition Lines of Communication (LOCs) and Supply Vehicles. Another major flaw in the Iraqi military strategy was the failure to focus attacks on the Coalition's LOCs and thin-skinned supply vehicles. The fast-moving Coalition combat forces depended on extended supply lines through areas that had not been fully cleared of enemy forces. However, the Iraqis apparently had no plan and made little or no attempt to interdict those lines of supply by having militia and other forces attack the thin-skinned tankers and other supply vehicles supporting the U.S. advance. Instead, the militia forces were directed to attack U.S. combat elements, particularly the tanks and APCs leading the U.S. advance.

Iraqi Defensive Operations Were Poorly Managed and Executed

Aside from being poorly planned, the Iraqi defense operations in OIF were also poorly managed and executed. These shortcomings resulted from the Iraqi forces' (1) dysfunctional command arrangements and practices, (2) poor situational awareness, (3) malpositioning on the battlefield, and (4) poor training.

---

[37] See Biddle testimony (2003). Saddam apparently believed that the destruction of Iraq's oil facilities would be bad for troop morale. See Woods et al. (2006).

[38] Some 22 Rumaila wells had been prepared for demolition, but only nine were actually detonated, resulting in only seven fires. See Biddle testimony (2003).

Iraqi Command Arrangements and Practices Were Dysfunctional

Iraq's Senior Decisionmakers Were Militarily Inept. Iraq's poor battlefield performance in OIF can be traced in part to the military incompetence of the country's top military and civilian leaders. Saddam's penchant for making key military decisions on his own and for populating Iraq's senior command positions with sycophantic and malleable relatives, fellow tribesmen, and other marginally competent loyalists significantly diminished the quality of Iraqi battlefield decisions. Poor decisions were allowed to stand because the officers who may have disagreed with a proposed course of action were deterred by their fear of Saddam from openly voicing their opposition.

As previously noted, Saddam had no military training or experience. Iraqi military officers who prided themselves as being professionals bemoaned the fact that their country's fate lay in the hands of a military naïf and incompetent whose ill-considered decisions and adventures had led their nation and military establishment into one disaster after another. A Regular Army colonel described the results of Saddam's decisionmaking as follows: "We are already used to his mistakes from the Iran-Iraq war and Kuwait. . . . Every plan of Saddam was a disaster."[39]

Saddam's immediate subordinate commanders were also largely unschooled in military affairs. Of the four regional commanders Saddam appointed in mid-March 2003 to manage the defense of Iraq, none had significant military backgrounds or competence. Saddam's cousin, Ali Hassan Al Majid ("Chemical Ali"), for example, was appointed to command Iraqi forces in Basra and the southern region of Iraq. Although slavishly loyal to Saddam and expert at ruthlessly repressing indigenous opponents, Ali was considered "militarily inept" at conventional conflict.[40] Saddam's son Qusay, who was given the most important regional command, the defense of Baghdad and its surrounding governorates, also lacked any significant military credentials.

Other senior regime officials were dismissive of Qusay's intelligence and leadership ability. They described him as "ambitious," "dis-

---

[39] Peterson and Ford (2003), pp. 1 and 12.

[40] Martin (2003).

trustful," and "fawning," and believed he had been given more responsibility then he could handle.[41] Many of Qusay's subordinates also held him in low esteem. The former commander of the Nebuchadnezzar Republican Guard Division commented that Qusay "never took any information seriously. He would just mark on the map. He thought most of us were clowns."[42]

Qusay's military shortcomings were manifest in his inept handling of a Republican Guard armored unit deployed to defend Baghdad. As American forces drove toward the city, Qusay gave the unit's commander a new, handwritten order every morning requiring the commander to reposition his tanks. According to Colonel Raaed Faik, each new order contradicted the one before, which infuriated the local commanders. Moreover, every time the tanks moved from their revetted and camouflaged positions, they became more exposed and a "few more" were discovered and destroyed by Coalition air strikes.[43]

Colonel Faik also reported that Qusay had ordered another commander to disable all 36 of his tanks for fear that they would fall into the hands of Kurdish militias located hundreds of miles to the north. In Colonel Faik's words, "These were the orders of an imbecile. Qusay was like a teenager playing a video war game."[44]

These criticisms were echoed by other Iraqi officers, who tended to blame Saddam and his sons, Qusay and Uday, for Iraq's poor battlefield decisions.

Even Tactical Battlefield Decisions Were Made in Baghdad. The pernicious effects of this absence of professionalism at the top echelons of the Iraqi chain of command were intensified by the fact that Saddam and his immediate subordinates exercised fine-grained control over military operations in Iraq. Decisions that in other military organizations would have been left to lower-echelon commanders were routinely made at higher headquarters. As previously mentioned, Baghdad

---

[41] Duelfer (2004), p. 22.

[42] Duelfer (2004), p. 67.

[43] Zucchino (2003), p. 1.

[44] Zucchino (2003), p. 1.

controlled the demolition of bridges and the subordination and positioning of military units. Indeed, even Iraqi corps commanders lacked the authority to move their units or blow up bridges without the prior approval of Baghdad.

Saddam's fear of military coups led him to direct that no significant armored or infantry element could be moved without the explicit permission of headquarters.[45] All decisions had to come from the top down. Further complicating the situation, Baghdad sometimes ordered the movement of units and even whole divisions without the knowledge or approval of the local corps commander.

Because Iraqi generals could exercise so little initiative in the command of their forces, they were denied the flexibility to adjust their defensive dispositions as they believed the battlefield situation dictated. In the view of Republican Guard II Corps Commander General Hamdani, Baghdad's tight control deprived commanders at all levels of the "freedom to move [and] disabled them from working as expected in crucial moments. Everybody was just waiting for orders." Moreover, there was little if any discussion between echelons about the possible risks or advantages of alternative courses of action. As General Hamdani put it, "The exaggeration in military discipline deprived the officers [of] the ability to discuss. There was no decisionmaking process, but only the carrying out [of] orders, even for [the] high levels. High-ranking officers didn't have enough authority."[46]

One consequence of this top-down decision process is that sometimes no decisions came down from Baghdad.[47] Because each

---

[45] According to the Duelfer (2004, p. 93) report, "No piece of military equipment could be moved—even for repair—by a [Republican Guard] brigade, division, or corps commander without the prior written permission of Qusay through the RG Secretariat."

[46] General Hamandi opined that this had been a weak point in the Iraqi Army since 1948, when it was called a "no orders" army. (Interview with Lieutenant General Hamdani, 2004.)

[47] Some officers reported receiving no orders during the entire duration of OIF. For example, Colonel Diar Abed, a wing commander at Rashid Air Base in southern Baghdad, stated that his unit "had no orders. We just stayed in the base and waited. I thought, 'I am losing my country, why don't they give us orders?' The leaders at the base didn't know anything" (Moore, 2003, p. A1).

of Iraq's rival forces responded only to directives from on high, commanders were paralyzed with indecision in the absence of orders from the regime leadership. As one Republican Guard general put it, "Initiative was discouraged. . . . No one dared to make decisions."[48]

Normal Chains of Command Were Disrupted. The Iraqi command arrangements to meet the Coalition attack were last-minute and disruptive to the Iraqi military's normal chains of command. Perhaps because he still thought a war might be avoided, Saddam waited until mid-March, less than a week before the onset of OIF, to put in place a new, overall command structure for the defense of Iraq. He divided the country into four separate regional commands, each, as previously mentioned, to be headed by leaders of proven loyalty but of little if any military competence.[49] The imposition of this new command arrangement not only diminished the quality of Iraq's battlefield leadership but also displaced the existing chains of command between the corps commanders and Baghdad. The Republican Guard II Corps Commander believed that from a "military strategic point of view, dividing the country into four separate commands . . . was a strategic mistake."[50]

Established chains of command were also upset when Baghdad detached numerous Regular Army units from under their normal corps headquarters and attached them to other commands. Elements of Republican Guard and Regular Army divisions were also parceled out to other divisions in a last-minute attempt to bolster local defenses. The movement and cross-attachment of units to new headquarters generally had a disorienting and debilitating effect on the combat effectiveness of the units involved.

There Was No Unity of Command or Battlefield Coordination. Saddam's paranoia about coups and other internal threats undermined the Iraqi defensive forces' unity of command and diminished their ability to coordinate on the battlefield. The diverse force structure that Saddam had deliberately created to fend off any common

---

[48] Zucchino (2003), p. 1.

[49] This was not the first time Saddam had used the four-region command structure; he had also done so during Operation Desert Fox.

[50] Interview with Lieutenant General Hamdani (2004).

action against his regime militated against unity of effort. The fact that the Regular Army, Republican Guard, Special Republican Guard, Fedayeen Saddam, Ba'ath militia, and Al Quds Army had their own, separate chains of command and rarely, if ever, interacted with each other, inevitably segmented and weakened the Iraqi defensive effort.

The internal-security-inspired prohibition against unauthorized interactions between different corps commands or between corps commands and divisions not under the corps' direct control further undermined any unity of effort. As the Republican Guard II Corps Commander General Hamdani described it,

> Each level of command was planning for itself. There was no harmony, only artificial coordination; but in fact there were no joint battles. Each level was fighting with [its] own plans, in a separate · way, but within the general view of the command. The Regular Army, Republican Guard, Quds Army, and Ba'ath Party militias were all fighting in a separate pattern, as if there [were] no unified armed forces.[51]

Brigadier General Rasheed Islam Joubouri, who spent 34 years in Regular Army infantry units, highlighted the animosity that existed between the various Iraqi forces: "There was no coordination between these armies—they hate each other."[52]

Iraqis Had Warning of Hostilities, but Situational Awareness Was Poor

Iraqi leaders were not surprised by the timing of the Coalition attack, because of the numerous political and military indicators that showed hostilities to be imminent. However, once the fighting got under way,

---

[51] Interview with Lieutenant General Hamdani (2004). Major General Abed Mutlaq Jaburi, a former division commander who had been jailed by Saddam for conspiring against the regime, also emphasized the absence of cooperation: "There was no unity of command. There were five different armies being used, no cooperation, no coordination" (Coll, 2003, p. A1).

[52] Moore (2003), p. A1.

Iraqi civilian leaders and battlefield commanders were continually surprised because their situational awareness was so poor.

Iraqis Had Warning That War Was Coming. The Iraqis had ample warning that a Coalition attack was about to commence in March. Iraqi military and civilian leaders had followed the build-up of Coalition air and ground forces in Kuwait through their intelligence sources and through the accounts of Coalition preparations reported in the print media, on television, and on the Internet.[53] They realized that an attack was imminent when the UN inspectors were withdrawn from Iraq and the UN observers monitoring the Kuwait-Iraq border were also withdrawn. President Bush's 48-hour ultimatum to Saddam, the bulldozing of the berms along the Kuwait-Iraqi border, and the increased reconnaissance overflights of Iraq were also indicators that hostilities would commence shortly.

According to the testimony of a senior Iraqi Intelligence Service (IIS) official, from August 2002 to early January 2003 the Iraqi military had accelerated defensive measures to prepare for an anticipated U.S. attack. Such measures included moving and hiding military equipment and weapons. Army commanders "at bases throughout Iraq were ordered to identify alternative locations and to transfer equipment and heavy machinery to off-base locations, taking advantage of farms and homes to hide items."[54] Ammunition stocks were also extensively dispersed. As war became closer, divisions moved out of their normal garrisons to survival positions.

At least one Iraqi commander made extensive early preparations. The Republican Guard II Corps Commander reports that, on his own initiative, he began preparing alternative positions for the divisions under his command as early as three months before the start of the war. General Hamdani claimed that he prepared almost 7,000 new fighting positions (some 1,500 per division) for the four divisions

---

[53] A field-grade Republican Guard officer stated that Iraq also "collected reliable tactical intelligence against U.S. forces in Kuwait and even knew when Operation Iraqi Freedom would start." One senior officer underlined "how important the Internet was to their understanding of general threat capabilities" (Duelfer, 2004, p. 32).

[54] Duelfer (2004), p. 65.

he commanded.[55] Ammunition for six months of fighting was accumulated, and these munitions, along with food, fuel, and other supplies, were distributed to new locations. All these preparations were "based on the anticipation" that war would break out after February 15, 2003."[56] General Hamdani, however, may have been an exception, because other Iraqi commanders appear to have been far less conscientious in the preparation of their units for battle.

General Hamdani also reported that the beginning of the war was not a "surprise" to him, and that his forces were on maximum alert as of March 20:

> The fall of the first missile on Baghdad on March 20 wasn't a surprise, because one day earlier, the defense alert system informed us of spotting 30 air targets on the sides of Baghdad. So we were on highest degree of readiness. Next day, there was one missile, followed by many missiles. So the beginning wasn't a surprise.[57]

Iraqi Situational Awareness Seemed Poor from the Outset. Saddam's understanding of the threat confronting his regime remained cloudy, even after the start of hostilities. Saddam's former advisers have suggested that he never concluded that the United States would attempt to overthrow his regime with an invasion.[58] He apparently continued to believe, even up to the first days of April, that Iraqi forces would put up a defense sufficient to force some kind of political settlement.

The persistence of this misperception was due to Saddam's and his Baghdad colleagues' limited grasp of what was transpiring on the Iraqi battlefield. The Baghdad headquarters staff reportedly was able to provide scant information on Coalition operations to subordinate commands. Most tellingly, the deployment decisions emanating from Saddam, which will be discussed below, reflect a gross misreading of the lines of advance of U.S. forces.

---

[55] These fighting positions were earthen revetments carved out for armored vehicles.

[56] Interview with Lieutenant General Hamdani (2004).

[57] Interview with Lieutenant General Hamdani (2004).

[58] Duelfer (2004), p. 32.

Subordinate battlefield commanders also exhibited very poor situational awareness. Division commanders only discerned the arrival of U.S. forces when they made contact with their own units. Iraqi commanders believed that U.S. air assault landings had taken place, when none had occurred, and believed that the U.S. 4th Infantry Division was in Iraq, when it was not. Many Iraqi general officers, believing regime propaganda that Coalition forces were bogged down in southern Iraq, admitted to being shocked when U.S. troops entered Baghdad.

General Hamdani, the Republican Guard II Corps Commander, who appeared to have the best grasp of the overall Coalition plan of attack, was frequently late in understanding the strength and location of the U.S. forces moving through his II Corps area of responsibility. General Hamdani also misread the fighting will of his own forces, admitting: "I had a mistaken idea that our forces will fight with high spirit and for [a] long time."[59]

Why Iraqi Situational Awareness Was So Poor. Several reasons seem to explain this poor situational awareness:

- The sources on which the Iraqi leaders depended for most of their intelligence—the non-Iraqi media and the Internet—provided only limited and largely dated information on U.S. troop movements and operations.[60]
- Because of U.S. air supremacy, no Iraqi aircraft flew in OIF. Iraqi leaders received information on the advance of U.S. forces from Iraqi units in contact with those forces and from Iraqi personnel along the route of march toward Baghdad. However, without an aerial surveillance and reconnaissance capability, they had difficulty gauging the depth, strength, and direction of march of the attacking U.S. formations.
- The Iraqi leaders' view of the American advance was also distorted by their assumption that U.S. forces would have to occupy the cities on their route of march. The optimistic reports from local Ba'ath Party officials and commanders, that the cities U.S. forces

---

[59] Interview with Lieutenant General Hamdani (2004).

[60] Duelfer (2004), p. 32.

had deliberately bypassed were still holding out, misled Iraqi leaders into believing that the American advance was stalled.[61]

- Saddam and other Iraqi leaders adopted countermeasures to reduce the threat of air attacks to their persons and headquarters' staffs that undoubtedly reduced their situational awareness. They abandoned their well-equipped headquarters and attempted to control operations from alternative command centers established in safe houses, schools, mosques, and other civilian facilities that they thought would be off limits to Coalition air attack. Saddam's avoidance of command posts, his constant movement from one safe house to another, and his refusal to use the telephone almost certainly impaired his ability both to acquire up-to-date pictures of the battlefield situation and to make timely decisions about force dispositions and bridge destruction.

- The "culture of lying" seems to also have carried over to the battlefield. Iraqi commanders were still wary about conveying "bad news" to Baghdad.[62] The Nebuchadnezzar Republican Guard Division Commander, for example, said that he continuously passed false information on to Qusay, the Republican Guard overseer:

> We pretended to have victory, and we never provided true information as it is here on the planet earth. Qusay always thought he'd gain victory. Any commander who spoke the truth would lose his head.[63]

- Once the war began, the U.S. "joint campaign was so decisive and so fast [in] getting to Baghdad that the regime's situational awareness was destroyed." This was the view of Lieutenant General David McKiernan, Commander, 3rd Army and CFLCC.

---

[61] Woods et al. (2006), pp. 130–131.

[62] According to the testimony of former senior Iraqi officers: "The few commanders who realized how desperate the situation had become were afraid to relay honest battlefield assessments up the chain of command." As one former general put it: "It was well known that President Hussein did not care to receive bad news" (Zucchino, 2003, p. 1).

[63] Duelfer (2004), p. 67.

The Iraqis "didn't know where we were; they didn't know where their own forces were; they hadn't had time to set a very deliberate Baghdad urban defense."[64]

Coalition deception operations also may have contributed to the poor Iraqi situational awareness, but this effect is difficult to document. The Iraqi II Corps Commander seems to have taken seriously at least one of the five simultaneous diversionary attacks that V Corps mounted to mask where the corps' main effort would cross the Euphrates River (north or south of Karbala), but these limited-objective attacks did not dissuade him from believing that an advance north of Karbala would be the main axis of attack.[65] General Franks believes that the deception operation conducted by an American officer code named "April Fool" kept the better part of 13 enemy divisions focused on defending against a U.S. 4th Infantry Division attack from the north.[66] Again, the evidence concerning the success of this deception is mixed: Although the bulk of the Regular Army divisions remained in the north along the Green Line facing the Kurdish Peshmerga militia and U.S. Special Operations units, the two Republican Guard divisions located in the north, the Adnan Mechanized and Nebuchadnezzar Infantry Divisions, moved south before the outbreak of hostilities.[67] Several Regular Army divisions also eventually moved south to strengthen the defense of Baghdad.[68]

Iraqi Forces Were Poorly Positioned for Defense

Whether because of poor situational awareness, strategic miscalculation, or command ineptitude, Iraqi forces in crucial instances were not

---

[64] See Interview with Lieutenant General David D. McKiernan, Commander, 3rd Army and CFLCC, "The Invasion of Iraq: An Oral History," *Frontline*, PBS, posted March 9, 2004. Online at http://www.pbs.org/wgbh/pages/frontline/shows/invasion/interviews/mckiernan.html (as of February 27, 2004).

[65] Interview with Lieutenant General Hamdani (2004). For a discussion of the five simultaneous attacks, see Fontenot, Degen, and Tohn (2004), pp. 258–261.

[66] See Franks (2004), pp. 434–436 and 500–501.

[67] See Fontenot, Degen, and Tohn (2004), pp. 212, 248, 252, 263, 296, 301, and 330.

[68] See Welsh (2004), and Peterson and Ford (2003), p. 12.

positioned well for an effective defense. As discussed earlier, Iraqi Regular Army forces were largely positioned to fight Kurds and Iranians; they were not positioned to meet an invasion from Kuwait. But malpositioning was evident in later stages of the conflict as well.

The Karbala Gap Was Lightly Defended. The Iraqi Republican Guard II Corps Commander believed that the main axis of the U.S. attack toward Baghdad was along the approach west of the Euphrates River and further realized that Karbala was the "neck of the bottle": Once U.S. forces had passed that point, they intended "to advance to Baghdad, moving towards Usfiyah, the airport, and then the presidential palaces."[69] General Hamdani's view that the Karbala Gap constituted the key potential bottleneck to the U.S. advance was fully shared by U.S. planners and commanders.[70]

Yet, Baghdad not only refused to sanction the reinforcement of Karbala but also ordered that Iraqi forces be pulled back from that area because they were thought to be too vulnerable in the terrain west of the Euphrates River.[71] As a consequence, U.S. forces found "the Karbala Gap lightly defended."[72] Lieutenant General William Scott Wallace, the U.S. V Corps Commander, was surprised that the Iraqis were not defending the Karbala Gap in "any strength at all": "Were I the enemy, I would have at least had something that was defending north of the Karbala Gap to deny that avenue of approach to us." As General Wallace described it, "the advance through the Karbala Gap, once we actually got through the rough terrain, went very rapidly, all

---

[69] Interview with Lieutenant General Hamdani (2004).

[70] "Virtually every American army officer knew about the gap from war games and exercises at places as far afield as Fort Hood, Texas, and Grafenwohr, Germany, because the city of Karbala represented the gateway to Baghdad" (Murray and Scales, 2003, pp. 203–204).

[71] See Frontline Transcript (2004). One senior Iraqi officer said Qusay had ordered the Republican Guard regiments to withdraw from the desert west of the capital to Baghdad. He went on to say that these soldiers, who were vital to the city's defense, then took off their uniforms and went home. See Fisk (2003).

[72] Fontenot, Degen, and Tohn (2004), p. 283.

the way up to Objective Peach, which is the next bridge crossing site over the Euphrates River."[73]

Saddam Ordered Forces to Redeploy to Face a Phantom Attack from the West. Perhaps the most wrongheaded positioning of Iraqi forces occurred on April 2, when Saddam ordered his commanders to move the Al-Nida Republican Guard Armored Division, which was defending the southeastern approaches to Baghdad to a position northwest of the capital to meet a U.S. attack from that direction.[74] Saddam's order was conveyed by the Iraqi Defense Minister, General Al Ta'i, at a meeting in Baghdad attended by Qusay, the Regular Army chief of staff, the Al Quds Army chief of staff, the Republican Guard chief of staff, and the commanders of the Republican Guard I and II Corps.

At the meeting, the defense minister disclosed that Saddam had concluded that the U.S. units closing in on the capital city from the south were simply part of "a strategic deception" and that the real attack on Baghdad would "be from the north," conducted by U.S. forces "coming from the western front" (i.e., Jordan).[75]

Saddam's remarkable finding reflected the extreme poverty of his situational awareness. It came at the point when the U.S. 3rd Division forces had already moved through the Karbala Gap and crossed the Euphrates River at Objective Peach and U.S. Marine troops were approaching Baghdad along the Tigris River valley.

The Republican Guard II Corps Commander, General Hamdani, objected to both the assessment of the threat and the accompanying order. He stated that his troops were in contact with the advancing American forces on several fronts (including near Karbala) and that the U.S. lines of march were indeed coming from the south. He briefed the assembled officers on the various axes of the U.S. advance and

---

[73] See Interview with Lieutenant General William Scott Wallace, Commander, V Corps, "The Invasion of Iraq: An Oral History," *Frontline*, PBS, posted March 9, 2004. Online at http://www.pbs.org/wgbh/pages/frontline/shows/invasion/interviews/wallace.html (as of February 27, 2004).

[74] The defense of the northern approaches to Baghdad was the immediate responsibility of the Republican Guard I Corps Commander.

[75] Interview with Lieutenant General Hamdani (2004).

emphasized that the "weak point" of the defense of Baghdad was the southwest corner.[76]

The defense minister told General Hamdani that no discussion was permitted, because this was a "message from the president" and that all commanders should start moving their troops to meet an attack from the north, beginning at 5 a.m. the next day, April 3.

Demonstrating how loath even the most senior Iraqi officers and officials were to contradict Saddam Hussein, General Hamdani reports that, when the other attendees at the meeting were asked for their views, "no one supported [my] opinion. . . . The Republican Guard chief of staff supported the view of the high command, that the attack will come from the north, [and] said that [I] was mistaken, and [that] we should work fast to implement the decision of the high command— to move the troops and focus on the north of Baghdad, not on the south."[77]

The Republican Guard II Corps Commander asked to be excused, on the grounds that "my army was fighting two battles, one on [the] Euphrates, the other on [the] Tigris River. I had to go, but I said clearly to . . . [Qusay] and all the audience, that if we don't defend fiercely in Karbala and send more than one division there this night, then the fate of Baghdad will be determined within the coming 48 hours."[78] But General Hamdani's own situational awareness was lagging at this

---

[76] Lieutenant General Hamdani told the officers that his description of the likely course of the U.S. advance on Baghdad "was not a personal speculation," but was "the exact words of Israeli Prime Minister Ariel Sharon to President Bush," which he "had read on the Internet about six weeks ago." After hearing Lieutenant General Hamdani, Qusay asked him, almost in a whisper, "Are you sure of what you are saying?" Hamdani answered, "Yes, as I'm sure that I'm talking with you now" (Interview with Lieutenant General Hamdani, 2004).

[77] When asked by his interviewer why his colleagues had reacted as they had, Lieutenant General Hamdani avoided criticism by stating the "all there in the audience were competent, experienced, and patriotic officers, but maybe for the reasons of military discipline, or there has been some confusion in their strategic views, so there were no measures taken to rectify this vision." Lieutenant General Hamdani believed that Qusay was convinced by his presentation: "I saw it in his face. When he told me to move the troops from my army to the army defending north of Baghdad, he was saying it [was] not a[n] order from him, but . . . an order he [was] obliged to obey. . . ." (Interview with Lieutenant General Hamdani, 2004).

[78] Interview with Lieutenant General Hamdani (2004).

point, because the opportunity to defend effectively at the Karbala Gap had already passed.

General Hamdani did not fully comply with Saddam's order; instead, he hedged against what he knew to be the real avenue of attack by keeping some of his force near Musaib, northwest of Karbala. But the order did force the Iraqi units designated for repositioning to abandon their prepared defensive positions and maneuver in broad daylight.

One Republican Guard unit (most probably attached to the Al-Nida Armored Division) that was ordered to give up "good defensive positions south of Baghdad on April 3" and move north, apparently abandoned their armor and other heavy weapons in the process. Amer Na'ama Abed, a Republican Guard major in the unit, recalled: "We couldn't believe it. Our artillery was ready, the tanks, everything was ready for battle." But following the order to move, "Guns and tanks were left in the open. We only carried with us rifles, launchers and guns, which we managed to take in a hurry." Major Abed and his fellow officers found the move so inexplicable that they suspected that they had been betrayed by commanders who had been paid off by the Americans.[79]

Iraqi Forces Were Poorly Trained

Coalition warfighters were surprised by how poorly trained their Iraqi opponents appeared. This lack of training was reflected in the Iraqi forces' inability to carry out basic military operations. Among other shortcomings, the Iraqi forces appeared unable to (1) coordinate supporting arms and to maneuver, (2) exploit cover and concealment, and (3) shoot accurately.

Inability to Coordinate Supporting Arms and to Maneuver. The inability of the Iraqi Republican Guard and Regular Army forces to carry out basic military operations testified to their lack of training. Lieutenant General James Conway, Commander of the 1st Marine

---

[79] According to Major Abed, commanders under Saddam "were paid extraordinary sums of money to gain their trust and allegiance to the regime. They were given money, palaces, and land. In my opinion, the Americans used the same method. I believe that money was the reason why most commanders succumbed" ("Treachery: How Iraq Went to War Against Saddam," *London Sunday Times*, January 11, 2004).

Expeditionary Force in OIF, characterized the resistance put up by the Republican Guard and Regular Army as "not terribly effective." As General Conway saw it,

> Any army should have the ability to coordinate its supporting arms, its defensive positions, its long range fires with its close range fires, [et cetera]. And that simply didn't happen. I can't cite you a single [instance] where we would qualify [the resistance] as being very effective.[80]

The V Corps Commander, Lieutenant General Wallace, had much the same view of the Iraqi resistance:

> I don't think it was very good. It did not seem to be well coordinated. It didn't seem to be very well led. . . . They never indicated, or in very, very few circumstances did they ever indicate or demonstrate[,] a capability to mass their artillery fires. They didn't seem to be able to maneuver with any degree of authority on the battlefield.[81]

Inability to Effectively Exploit Cover and Concealment. To protect their heavy Republican Guard units, the Iraqis widely dispersed their tanks and APCs in revetments and also attempted to hide them in palm groves. They moved their equipment around so that equipment found during the day "might not be there that night."[82] However, Stephen Biddle found that Iraqi attempts to protect their forces from air and ground attack generally fell short of what was needed. The Iraqis were able to provide some concealment against air attacks for some units, "[b]ut they were much less successful in creating adequate cover. And they were systematically unable to combine cover, concealment, and an adequate field of fire for their own weapons." The horse-

---

[80] Interview with Lieutenant General James T. Conway, "The Invasion of Iraq: An Oral History," *Frontline*, PBS, posted March 9, 2004. Online at http://www.pbs.org/wgbh/pages/frontline/shows/invasion/interviews/conway.html (as of February 27, 2004).

[81] Interview with Lieutenant General Wallace (2004).

[82] Interview with Lieutenant General Wallace (2004).

shoe revetments they dug for many of their armored vehicles provided little, if any, protection from standoff M1A1 tank fire.[83]

The Iraqis also made little use of concealment and cover in built-up areas. Even though the Special Republican Guard had apparently received some training for urban warfare, it demonstrated little capacity for such fighting in Baghdad. The Special Republican Guard's "prepared positions were almost entirely outdoors, typically in shallow foxholes dug along the roadside or in simple sandbag emplacements on building roofs or at intersections." The Special Republican Guard tanks in Baghdad "were often simply parked in the open at major intersections, with no effort at cover or concealment."[84] Thus, even the Iraqi units that had reportedly received some training for urban combat often performed as though they had had no training at all in this type of warfare.

The tactics used by the Fedayeen Saddam and Ba'ath Party militias and foreign jihadists reflected almost a complete absence of conventional military training. The paramilitaries were lightly armed; their principal weaponry was AK-47s, grenades, rocket-propelled grenades, and mortars. Nearly always on the tactical offensive, these paramilitary units made little if any use of concealment or cover, electing typically to attack U.S. armored elements in the open and taking huge losses in the process. Apparently undaunted by U.S. military prowess, they persisted in their attacks. Their near-suicidal behavior in battle may have partly been a function of their ignorance about the consequences of frontally attacking armored vehicles in open terrain.

As Stephen Biddle described it, "Iraqi tactics could charitably be described as self-defeating":

> Much of the close combat in OIF took the form of Iraqi paramilitaries charging Coalition armored vehicles on the outskirts of Iraqi cities using civilian sport utility vehicles, pickup trucks, minivans, and even bicycles. These were typically simple frontal assaults, fully exposed, with no apparent attempt to coordinate

---

[83] Biddle testimony (2003).

[84] Biddle testimony (2003).

movement with suppressive fire, use terrain for cover, or employ smoke or other obscurants. Moreover, they were usually directed at Coalition heavy armored units; Iraqi paramilitaries appear to have systematically avoided softer-skinned command or logistical elements in order to seek out Coalition tanks and infantry fighting vehicles.[85]

According to General Wallace, the paramilitaries and the Iraqi civilians they coerced into joining their formations

Appeared to have been given instructions by someone, in some kind of formal military sense: where to stand, where to point their weapons, how to provide mutual support. But there was no apparent—what we would refer to as tactical leadership—in the organizations. And there was no apparent ability or intention to innovate beyond what they had been told to do.[86]

Inability to Shoot Accurately. Coalition forces were also fortunate in that Iraqi shooting accuracy was so poor. This bad marksmanship was apparent in both Iraqi regular military and militia units, and it was frequently commented on by U.S. forces. Among U.S. Marine units, "everyone on the front lines" gradually developed "skepticism about, if not disdain for, Iraqi marksmanship."[87] Marines described the typical Iraqi firing routine as "spray and pray."

Stephen Biddle has documented this "very poor" Iraqi marksmanship:

Against the 3rd Infantry's 3rd Brigade in Baghdad, Iraqi paramilitaries attained a hit rate of under ten percent for rocket[-]propelled grenades (RPGs) fired at ranges of under 500 meters. At Objective Montgomery west of Baghdad, an elite Republican

---

[85] Biddle testimony (2003). Also see Stephen Biddle et al., "Iraq and the Future of Warfare," briefing, Strategic Studies Institute, U.S. Army War College, Carlisle, Pa., August 18, 2003.

[86] Interview with Lieutenant General Wallace (2004).

[87] Bing West and Major General Ray L. Smith, U.S. Marine Corps (USMC) (Ret.), *The March Up*, New York: Bantam Books, 2003, p. 144.

Guard tank battalion fired at least 16 T-72 main gun rounds at ranges of as little as 800-1000 meters at the fully exposed flanks of the U.S. 3-7 Cavalry's tanks and Bradley fighting vehicles— with zero hits at what amounted to point[-]blank range for weapons of this caliber. In fact, the nearest miss fell 25 meters short of the lead American troop commander's tank. Similar results are reported from American and British combatants throughout the theater of war, and across all Iraqi weapon types employed in OIF.[88]

One American commander suggested to the author that some of the Iraqi misses may have been intentional, that the Iraqi troops were making a token show of fighting, so as to avoid possible punishment from their commanders or Ba'athist overseers. Stephen Biddle, however, attributes the poor marksmanship to "radically substandard training" in weapons employment. Recalling his unit's poor marksmanship, a Republican Guard soldier who had been stationed in Kut, some 100 miles southeast of Baghdad, stated: "We never hit a single target . . . one mortar we shot killed about eight Iraqi civilians."[89]

As incongruous as it may appear in a country overflowing with ammunition and other munitions of all types, the Iraqi regular military and militiamen alike spent little if any time on the firing range. According to Stephen Biddle, "[m]ost Iraqi fighters had fired little or no live ammunition in the year prior to the war; some had never fired their weapons at all." He points to two Iraqi Regular Army units (the 2nd Division and 3rd Battalion, 11th Division) that held no live-fire training during the 12 months preceding OIF, and one (3rd Division) that had allowed each soldier only four rounds of ammunition in one live-fire exercise. "Even the Baghdad Republican Guard division held only a single live fire exercise with just ten rounds for every soldier in the year leading up to the war." [90]

---

[88] See Biddle testimony (2003).

[89] Walt (2003).

[90] Biddle contrasts the Iraqi troop's paucity of firing-range munitions to the 2,500 or more rounds of training ammunition that is accorded to each soldier annually in a typical U.S.

Iraqis Had to Operate with Reduced Inventories of Old Equipment

The Iraqi forces were further disadvantaged by much of their military equipment being old and inferior to that of the Coalition.

The armor, artillery, and other equipment losses Iraq had suffered in the 1991 Gulf War had been enormous. During the course of that conflict, the Iraqi military probably lost well over one-half of its prewar inventory of tanks and artillery tubes and over one-third of its inventory of APCs. In addition, the Iraqi ground forces are estimated to have lost many thousands of their trucks and possibly as much as one-half of their heavy equipment transports (HETs).[91]

By the time the Iraqi military entered its second war with the United States, it was a "suffering, weakened institution." As General Qahtan al-Tamimi, a 37-year Iraqi military veteran, put it: "Our army was systematically destroyed over time as no other army in history."[92]

Iraq was prevented from replacing these losses and its remaining largely old Soviet-designed armory with modern weapon systems by the sanctions that were imposed by the United Nations at the end of the Gulf War. Although some smuggling of spare parts and other military equipment reportedly occurred during the years leading up to OIF, it proved no substitute for Iraq being able to buy advanced equipment on the open market.[93]

Moreover, the number of spare parts that could be smuggled into the country still fell far short of Iraq's needs. According to one assessment, as much as 50 percent of Iraq's estimated inventory of main battle tanks, armored fighting vehicles and personnel carriers, towed

---

infantry unit. This disparity suggests that a typical American infantryman "had over 250 times as much target practice as even the best Iraqis" (Biddle testimony, 2003).

[91] Hosmer (2002), p. 181.

[92] May Ying Welsh "U.S. Trains Proxy to Quell Resistance," Aljazeera.Net, June 6, 2004. Online at http://english.aljazeera.net/NR/excres/554FAF3A-B267-427A-BQEC-54881BDEOA2E.ht (as of June 10, 2004).

[93] See "Armed Forces, Iraq," *Jane's Sentinel Security Assessment—The Gulf States,* January 13, 2003. Online at http://sentinel.janes.com/subscriber/sentinel/doc_view_print.jsp?K2DocKey=/content1/jane (as of January 20, 2004).

artillery pieces, multiple rocket launchers, and helicopters lacked needed spares.[94] Among other crucial missing items were new night-vision devices to replace the worn-out devices on Iraqi tanks. Iraq's infantry, mechanized, and armored divisions—except for the units of the Republican Guard—were assessed as having only 50 percent of their former combat effectiveness.[95] According to Iraqi commanders, the military's artillery batteries "were operating at 50 percent" of their normal capability.[96]

Coalition air operations in the no-fly zones during the years before OIF also significantly diminished Iraqi combat capabilities. Beginning in June 2002, Coalition air strikes on Iraq's integrated air defense system in the no-fly zones, including its surface-to-air missiles and their command and control, were stepped up, further degrading an already-impaired air defense network. Between March 1 and the March 20th start of the ground invasion, Coalition pilots flew some 4,000 strike and support sorties in the no-fly zones, destroying Iraqi radars, air defense guns, and fiber-optic links.[97]

The commander of missile air defenses for Baghdad lamented the inferiority of Iraq's military equipment:

> . . . my own ground-to-air missiles had a range of only 43 kilometers. . . . Their planes could detect our radar and fly faster than my missiles and then turn round and bomb my crews. So I would send only one battery to engage an American aircraft and [kept] the rest safe.[98]

---

[94] *Jane's Defence Weekly*, February 5, 2003. Online at http://www4.janes.com/K2/docprint.jsp?K2DocKey=/content1/janesdata/mags/jdw/history (as of January 29, 2007).

[95] The International Institute for Strategic Studies, *The Military Balance*, London: Oxford University Press, 2000–2001.

[96] Moore (2003), p. A1.

[97] Susann Chapman, "The 'War' Before the War," *Air Force Magazine*, February 2004, p. 52.

[98] Even using this tactic, the commander's missile crews still suffered 30 killed and another 40 wounded. Fisk (2003).

However, the fact is that the Iraqis rarely turned their radars on. The vast majority of Iraqi air-defense missiles fired in OIF were unguided.

CHAPTER FIVE
Poor Motivation and Morale Decisively Undermined the Iraqi Defense

Poor planning, leadership, training, and equipment contributed to the rapid Iraqi defeat. However, the prime reason for the lack of resistance was the Iraqi military's extremely poor motivation and morale. The vast majority of the officers and troops in the Regular Army, Republican Guard, and Special Republican Guard did little if any fighting, and they deserted their units before being engaged by Coalition ground forces. The reasons for this lack of fighting will and the high desertion rate were several: (1) the poor morale that existed prior to the outbreak of hostilities, (2) the widespread conviction that resistance was futile, (3) the absence of a belief in the cause, (4) the erosion of the previous barriers to desertion, and (5) the effect of U.S. air attacks.

Psychological operations (PSYOPS) and the rapid advance, technological supremacy, and firepower of U.S. ground forces also helped undermine the enemy's will to resist. The limited resistance that Coalition forces encountered came mainly from Iraqi militia units—the Saddam Fedayeen, the Ba'ath Party militia, and foreign jihadists—although small elements from various Iraqi Republican Guard and Regular Army units did fight. The entry of U.S. units into Baghdad and the fall of the capital, on April 9, brought an end to organized resistance.

Prewar Motivation and Morale Were Poor

Senior Iraqi officers, as well as rank-and-file troops, interviewed after the collapse of Saddam's regime report that the motivation and morale of Iraqi military forces were poor long before the first U.S. troops crossed the Iraqi border on March 20.[1] In the months leading up to the war, there were numerous reports of low morale and high desertion rates within Iraqi units. Iraqi military officers who fled to Europe in mid-2002, for example, claimed that more than a quarter of the estimated 375,000-man-strong Iraqi army was "missing from their posts as a result of poor and irregular pay, fear of bombing, and concern about potential purges."[2]

According to Colonel Abu Ala Zuhairi, who served 23 years in infantry air defense units, "the army was fed up and tired of fighting after three wars. The commanders received many presents, but the soldiers were starving."[3] Aside from poor pay and food, conscripts (who were mainly Shiites) were often badly mistreated by their Sunni officers.[4] They were apparently also mistrusted by their superiors, and so some troops were given only a single magazine of ammunition.[5]

To escape the poor food and other vicissitudes of military life, Iraqi soldiers constantly sought home leave to visit their families, requests that were often granted only after suitable bribes had been paid to their officers.[6] Whether because of desertions or recruitment problems, Regular Army units were significantly undermanned, some possessing as little as 40 percent or less of their authorized strength.[7]

A telling manifestation of the endemic poor morale in Iraqi units was the propensity of Iraqi troops to carry civilian clothing along with their military gear. The troops were preparing for their eventual deser-

---

[1]   Branigin (2003), p. A25.

[2]   See Ewen MacAskill and Julian Borger, "Iraq 'to Allow Arms Inspectors,'" *The Guardian Weekly* (London), May 2–8, 2002, p. 2.

[3]   Moore (2003), p. A1.

[4]   Slocombe (2003), p. A29.

[5]   Zucchino (2003), p. 1.

[6]   In some units, home leave was granted to personnel 10 days out of every month. See Leonard Wong, Thomas A. Kolditz, Raymond A. Millen, and Terrence M. Potter, *Why They Fight: Combat Motivation in the Iraq War*, Carlisle, Pa.: Strategic Studies Institute, U.S. Army War College, July 2003, p. 8.

[7]   Wong et al. (2003), p. 8.

tion even before the outbreak of hostilities. American officers reported finding piles of discarded uniforms when they overran abandoned Iraqi military positions.

Prewar morale within the senior ranks of the Iraqi officer corps was also poor. When Saddam told his senior officers in December 2002 that they might have to fight the United States without WMD, "military morale dropped rapidly."[8] Those Iraqi officers who had detailed information about U.S. capabilities had realized "that the imbalance in power between Iraq and the United States was so disparate that they were incapable of halting a U.S. invasion."[9]

Morale was also undermined by the "culture of lying" that permeated the military's ranks and by the disdain many officers held for the inept loyalists Saddam had placed in key command positions. The bureaucracy and widespread corruption that plagued the armed forces also diminished morale. General Hamdani stated that the

> . . . commitment to Iraqi military honor was weakened, due to economic sanctions. Administrative corruption was widely spread. One day the supervisor [Qusay] asked me about the behavior of our armed forces. I replied that there was [a] high level of bureaucracy; it was like a tumor.[10]

Some officers also made preparations to desert. Iraqi soldiers reported instances in which their officers ordered military vehicles spray-painted in nonmilitary colors, "intending to drive them home for personal use after deserting."[11]

---

[8]   Duelfer (2004), p. 65.

[9]   Duelfer (2004), p. 32.

[10] Interview with Lieutenant General Hamdani (2004).

[11] Zucchino (2003), p. 1.

Most Iraqis Saw Defeat as Inevitable

One fundamental reason the Iraqis chose not to fight in OIF was that both officers and enlisted personnel were convinced that any attempt at resistance would be futile. They believed that their diminished military forces would be no match for the technologically superior U.S. air and ground forces in conventional combat. Commanders who were veterans of the 1991 Persian Gulf War undoubtedly remembered the beating their Iraqi units had taken from fast-moving, better-equipped U.S. armored forces. Senior Iraqi commanders had also observed the devastating effects of U.S. air supremacy during Desert Storm and during the subsequent 12-year enforcement of the no-fly zones, and they realized that they would be unable to protect their forces from destruction by U.S. air attacks.

Thus, with the exception of Saddam Hussein and some of his immediate family members and political cohorts, pessimism about the possibility of successfully fending off a U.S. attack appears to have permeated all levels of the Iraqi military command structure. Even Saddam's former Minister of Defense, General Al Ta'i, thought the war would be lost rapidly:

> We knew the goal was to make the Regime fall. . . . We thought the forces would arrive in Baghdad or outside Baghdad in 20 days or a month. We accepted that the cities on the way would be lost. All commanders knew this and accepted it.[12]

Many members of the Republican Guard forces also thought resistance would be futile. Colonel A. T. Said, who commanded a 150-man engineering unit attached to the Republican Guard Hammurabi Division, testified that the Republican Guard troops he knew believed that war would be "madness": "We knew we would never fight. I thought the war would never start because it was madness."

Colonel Said went on to describe the cynicism of the sycophantic Republican Guard generals, who assured Saddam of military victory during televised meetings: "They told him we would fight any power

---

[12] Quoted in Duelfer (2004), p. 67.

in the world. When we heard this, we couldn't believe it. But then the generals told us, 'No, no—don't worry. Just keep quiet. Stay in your positions. It won't happen.'"[13]

Cynicism also permeated Saddam's private "pep rallies." On March 16, 2003, four days before the U.S. invasion, Saddam assembled some 150 of his general officers in an underground auditorium outside Baghdad for a pep talk. After exhorting his generals and delivering a tirade against the United States, Saddam opened the floor to comments. General Kareem Saadoun, an air force commander, stepped forward and proclaimed: "We are ready to fight for our land. . . . We hope there will be no war, but if it comes, we will be willing to die." Other senior officers spoke up in a similar vein, assuring Saddam of the good combat capability and fighting will of their units.

According to General Saadoun, all these officers were lying. Every one of them realized that their tanks, aircraft, and other weaponry were too old and decrepit to effectively confront U.S. forces: "We knew there was no way to fight the Americans," Saadoun said, "We knew we'd lose the war."[14]

In the view of one Iraqi colonel, the Iraqi armed forces were doomed to defeat from the outset, because they had never recovered from the beating they had taken in the 1991 Gulf War. According to the colonel:

> You can't fight with what was left. . . . and this war was not just about what you learn at the military academy—it is technological and we recognized that. . . . The Army believed that from the first bullet fired by the British in the south, it would lose.[15]

Lieutenant Colonel Amer Abdullah al-Rubaie echoed this pessimistic view, stating, "[The Coalition] didn't defeat the Iraqi Army

---

[13] David Blair, "145 of My 150 Men Fled, Says Guard Officer," *Telegraph (UK)*, filed April 14, 2003a.

[14] See quotes from interview with General Saadoun in Moore (2003), p. A1.

[15] Peterson and Ford, (2003), pp. 1 and 12.

because the army didn't fight. We knew we wouldn't win against a modern force."[16]

But some Iraqi officers thought Iraq's defeat would take longer than it did. Major Jaburi, who was a battalion commander in the Army's 2nd Infantry Division, knew defeat was inevitable but was surprised at its swiftness:

> But we were expecting that the war would last longer than it did. We were desperate when Baghdad fell so quickly. If we were not Muslims we would have done like the Japanese and committed suicide [but] . . . our religion forbids it.[17]

Brigadier General Hassen Jabani, who commanded a tank unit in the Republican Guard, reported that the day before U.S. air strikes on April 4 had turned his T-72 tanks into burning hulks, his soldiers had begun to desert in droves, believing that any attempt at defense was futile:

> Seventy percent of my soldiers went home. . . . I saw we had no chance to win. I let them go. We retreated without any fighting. It was no use. . . . Everybody knew we'd lose to the Americans.[18]

Sometimes, Iraqi commanders held meetings with their men, even in the midst of battle, to decide whether to fight or flee. Colonel Abdul Kareem Abdul Razzaq, whose unit was involved in the fighting at the Baghdad International Airport, recounted telling his men:

> The [U.S.] Air Force is bombing, there's a huge American Army coming we can't fight, [and] we are losing control. . . . We've been ordered to continue fighting. What do you think we should do?

---

[16] Susan Sachs, "A Former Iraqi Officer Denied His Old Post, Fumes at the U.S.," *The New York Times*, November 2, 2003, p. A12.

[17] Peterson and Ford (2003), pp. 1 and 12.

[18] Moore (2003), p. A1.

Colonel Abdul Razzaq reported that his men—the remaining 600 of his original 1,500 soldiers who had not deserted or been killed in the battle for the airport—were nearly unanimous in their decision to go home. "I gave the order to retreat. . . . If I had given the order for my soldiers to stay, they'd all be killed."[19]

Lack of Belief in the Justness and Necessity of the Cause

If defeat was inevitable, most of the officers and enlisted men of the Regular Army and the Republican Guard forces saw little or no reason to fight and die for Saddam and his regime. Even though they were dependent on Saddam for their positions and were the recipients of his cash bonuses and other largesse, many senior Iraqi officers apparently felt little loyalty toward the Iraqi leader, his sons, or the militarily incompetent relatives he had placed in many high commands. Although the senior officers feared Saddam, they did not respect him, in part because he kept dragging Iraq into costly wars. The previously discussed "culture of lying" that permeated the Iraqi senior officer corps' relationship with Saddam foreshadowed the problematic loyalty that would be accorded the Iraqi leader, once his removal appeared to be in the offing.

Iraqi officers also apparently did not believe that a Coalition victory over Saddam would be necessarily catastrophic for their own careers and livelihood. Some Iraqi officers did not expect Coalition forces to seize Baghdad or that Iraq would be "occupied." The Commander of the Nebuchadnezzar Republican Guard Division, for example, stated, "We thought the Coalition would go to Basrah, maybe to Amarra, and then the war would end."[20]

Others, while anticipating an occupation, probably did not expect the dissolution of the Iraqi military and the banning of most former general officers from positions in the new Iraqi military. Indeed, some officers assumed that they would keep their "privileged position in the

---

[19] Moore (2003), p. A1.

[20] Duelfer (2004), p. 67.

military even if it meant serving a new master."[21] Lieutenant Colonel
Amer Abdullah al-Rubaie, a Special Forces instructor and son of a
retired general, lamented the fact that he had not been called back to
duty at the end of the war as he had anticipated: "All of us thought that
we'd take our places again and help stabilize the situation."[22]

Many other officers no doubt understood that the demise of Saddam's regime would probably mark the end of their military careers.
However, there is little if any evidence that concerns about postwar
status motivated an appreciable numbers of Regular Army and Republican Guard officers to resist. For those regular military officers who
chose to stand and fight during OIF, the principal motivation appears
to have been their desire to uphold their nation's honor and their own
military honor by carrying out the duties assigned them.

Iraqi senior officers offered a variety of reasons for the decision
not to fight:

- Colonel Jamal Salem, who headed operations at a major supply
  base near Baghdad, stated, "We didn't work for Saddam Hussein,
  we worked for the country. . . . It was our job. I loved the army.
  . . . [Consequently] we had no fight with the Americans. When
  we heard they were in Baghdad, it was over for us."[23]
- General Ghanem Abdullah Azawi, an engineer in the Iraqi Regular Army air defense command, attributed the Iraqi refusal to fight
  to the fact that "The army didn't believe in it, because it wasn't
  a war, it was suicide." As the senior Iraqi commanders viewed it,
  "this war has no result, only death. Why should we fight to save
  Saddam? That's why most of the commanders told their soldiers
  not to fight, just withdraw."[24]
- Seeing the destruction of his equipment, the disarray of his leaders,
  and the desertion of his comrades in the final days of the war, Captain
  Ahmed Hassan, whose infantry unit was assigned to the defense of

---

[21] Sachs (2003), p. A12.

[22] Sachs (2003), p. A12.

[23] Moore (2003), p. A1.

[24] Branigin (2003), p. A25.

Kirkuk, said he simply had no incentive to fight: "I asked my commander, 'Why should I stay? The people behind me are retreating.' . . . I took off my high ranks and said goodbye to everything I'd known for 13 years."[25]

- Colonel Faik, who was also proud of his 12-year Republican Guard career, felt personally betrayed by his leaders and attributed the absence of fighting will to the shortcomings of the commanders at the top: "Professional soldiers can't fight without orders and inspiration from their leaders," he asserted. "But we had clowns for leaders. This is our tragedy." Colonel Faik went on to say how the soldiers used to hear Saddam say in his speeches: "Saddam is Iraq and Iraq is Saddam." But in the end, as Colonel Faik put it, "when the time came to fight for this guy who sends us unprepared to fight a superior American military, no one was willing to die for Saddam."[26]
- Colonel Said, whose unit was attached to the Republican Guard Hammurabi Division, claimed that the Republican Guard units that Saddam relied on most to defend his regime never had any intention of fighting for the Iraqi leader. According to Colonel Said, even before the combat began, most Republican Guard troops viewed Saddam with contempt and hatred. "We would say, 'Our leader is mad, mad, mad. And wants to cut all our throats.'"[27]

If officers had little positive motivation to fight for Saddam and his regime, Iraqi enlisted personnel apparently had even less. Interviews with some 30 Iraqi enemy prisoners of war (EPWs), largely from Regular Army units, uncovered no evidence that Iraqi enlisted personnel were motivated by considerations of Iraqi nationalism or the need to repel an American invasion force. Instead, the interviews showed that these Iraqi soldiers were motivated in the main by coercion, "the fear of retribution and punishment by Baath Party or Fedayeen Saddam if

[25] Moore (2003), p. A1.

[26] Zucchino (2003), p. 1.

[27] Blair (2003a).

they were found avoiding combat."[28] When Iraqi troops deserted, they invariably took their weapons with them to protect themselves from members of the Fedayeen Saddam death squads they might encounter in the rear areas.[29]

There was little small-unit cohesion within the squads and platoons in which the EPWs served, because unit cohesiveness was fragmented by tribal and regional differences. Moreover, the enlisted personnel found their officers to be "distant" and frequently tactically incompetent, particularly if they were political appointees. According to the analysis of these EPW interrogations,

> The ability of the Iraqi small unit leadership to invoke loyalty and influence up and down the command chain was almost completely lacking and unquestionably contributed to the disintegration of Iraqi Regular Army units in the face of advancing Coalition forces. . . . The Iraqi Regular Army appeared to be a poorly trained, poorly led, disparate group of conscripts who were more concerned with self-preservation and family ties than defending their country.[30]

The Previous Barriers to Desertion Eroded

Military discipline within the Iraqi military was largely maintained by fear. Officers closely controlled their troops, and even slight infractions tended to be severely punished. As a senior officer captured during the 1991 Gulf War put it,

> Iraqi military discipline, especially with enlisted soldiers, is based on fear. Soldiers are not motivated by the leadership, they are distrusted and are not taught to have initiative. . . . Even in complet-

---

[28] Except for a lieutenant colonel and a lieutenant, all the EPWs were lower-ranking enlisted Iraqi soldiers. Two sergeants claimed to have served in Republican Guard or Special Republican Guard units. See Wong et al. (2003), pp. 5, 7, and 9.

[29] Wong et al. (2003), p. 7.

[30] Wong et al. (2003), pp. 8–9.

ing the simplest task, Iraqi soldiers are closely supervised and are treated as if they were mentally deficient.[31]

The behavior of Iraqi officers was also monitored, both by their superiors and by the members of the Special Security Organization and the Directorate of General Military Intelligence who were embedded in the Republican Guard and Regular Army divisions.

During the 1991 Gulf War, the supervisory mechanism that enforced discipline in Iraq's military forces often broke down, which permitted large-scale desertions and battlefield surrenders.[32] In OIF, the barriers to desertion disappeared entirely, for two reasons: (1) The threat of eventual punishment dissolved, and (2) discipline was no longer enforced.

The Threat of Eventual Punishment Was No Longer Credible

During OIF, the threat of eventual punishment, which had previously deterred would-be deserters from fleeing their units, was no longer credible. In previous wars, deserters had run the risk of being hunted down by Saddam's security services and severely punished. During the Iran-Iraq War, deserters were frequently executed, sometimes along with the members of their families. While battlefield executions were relatively rare during the 1991 Persian Gulf War, would-be deserters still had to worry about both the possibility of capture by the "death squads" Saddam had positioned behind Iraqi lines and the risks of eventual arrest and punishment even after the war was over.[33]

In the days preceding OIF, the prospect of punishment remained a barrier to desertion for some Iraqis troops, because such an action could sometimes result in the cutting off of an ear.[34] However, once OIF was under way, the prospect that Saddam's regime would be

---

[31] Hosmer (2002), p. 121.

[32] Some 40 percent of the Iraqi forces in the KTO deserted before the Coalition ground offensive commenced. Most of the remaining Iraqi Regular Army forces in the KTO surrendered at their first opportunity. See Hosmer (2002).

[33] Hosmer (2002).

[34] Sachs (2003), p. A12.

ousted eliminated the threat of eventual punishment. Deserters still had to worry about evading Fedayeen Saddam militiamen who might attempt to intercept them on their way home, but this threat diminished in the absence of set battle lines and as the Fedayeen Saddam became engaged in the fighting—or deserted themselves.

Iraqi troops apparently delayed their desertion until they had evidence that Coalition forces had indeed invaded the country and seemed intent on ousting the regime. Some Iraqis saw the targets of U.S. air strikes as indicators of Coalition intent. When Saddam's palaces were spared in the bombing, some Iraqis questioned the Coalition's resolve to topple the Iraqi leader. However, when Ba'ath Party and other regime headquarters were struck, some of the Iraqi troops in and around urban centers apparently became more convinced that Saddam would be ousted. This, among other reasons, explains why desertions greatly increased as the demise of Saddam's regime appeared to come closer.

Iraqi forces chose desertion over surrender, not only because they wanted to return to their homes and take care of their families but also because at least some of them were uncertain about their treatment should they be captured. Changing into civilian clothes was the principal stratagem for avoiding capture.[35] Many soldiers, anticipating possible desertion, carried street clothes with them, sometimes worn under their military garb. Those who did not do so had attempted to beg or borrow clothes from local residents.[36]

For some Republican Guard troops, surrender was not an option. A Republican Guard infantryman stated that he and his fellow soldiers were convinced that it would be dangerous to surrender to the Americans:

---

[35] After hearing that U.S. forces were arresting men wearing combat boots, deserters discarded their military footwear and walked in bare feet or newly acquired sandals. See Terry McCarthy, "What Ever Happened to the Republican Guard?" *Time Magazine*, May 12, 2003, p. 41.

[36] One soldier reportedly offered to exchange his AK-47 weapon for a shirt and a pair of pants. McCarthy (2003), p. 40.

We believed that if you were wearing the uniform of the Republican Guard, the Americans would kill you. So we just took off our uniforms and put on civilian clothes.[37]

The infantrymen's officers didn't attempt to stop them, because many of them were doing the same thing.[38]

Officers No Longer Enforced Discipline

Probably an even more important reason for the massive Iraqi desertions was that the officers who were supposed to enforce discipline, deserted themselves or, as was the case most frequently, sanctioned, facilitated, and even ordered the desertion of their troops. Because they believed that Saddam's regime did not merit defending and that resistance would be futile, many Iraqi generals and other senior officers—whose duty it was to lead their troops into battle and prevent desertions in their units—decided to forsake these basic military responsibilities.

In OIF, the Iraqi troops typically did not find their officers to be barriers to either desertion or surrender. None of the Iraqi officers and infantrymen interviewed by one journalist could recall any soldier from their units being punished for attempted desertion. Instead, commanders turned a blind eye to such behavior and frequently deserted themselves.[39]

The 30 or so Iraqi prisoners of war interviewed in April 2003 indicated that their "officers permitted surrender, sometimes by their own desertion, sometimes by benign neglect." In the sample interviewed, which consisted mainly of enlisted personnel, the surrender decisions had been made by small groups of soldiers and were not the result of capitulation orders from higher headquarters. When one of two Iraqi officers in the sample was asked why he had not forced his men to fight, he responded, "As a man before Allah, that would have been the wrong thing to do." The officer and his unit had been charged with defending

---

[37] Mark MacKinnon, "Firepower Broke Iraqi Army, Survivor Says," *Toronto Globe and Mail*, April 23, 2003, p. 11.

[38] MacKinnon (2003), p. 11.

[39] See Walt (2003).

the perimeter of an oil field, but had to do so without a map, a plan, or communication with higher headquarters.[40]

Even as American forces sped toward Baghdad, Iraqi officers facilitated desertions by granting their soldiers "leave to visit their families."[41] Some senior officers actually prompted the desertion of their troops by telling them to go home. In their interviews, commanders reported that they "ordered their soldiers to defend their homes and families, but did not tell them to take offensive action against Americans."[42]

Massive desertions occurred within even the most elite Republican Guard units as senior commanders proved unwilling to push their troops toward inevitable slaughter by technologically superior U.S. forces. The commander of a Republican Guard armored brigade reportedly was ordered on April 4 to abandon his tanks south of Baghdad and "have his men change into civilian clothes." Minibuses took the troops to their home base near the northern city of Mosul, "where the soldiers simply quit and went home."[43]

Air Attacks Had a Devastating Effect on the Iraqi Capability and Will to Fight

Aside from the very considerable physical damage they inflicted, U.S. and other Coalition air attacks had major psychological effects on Iraqi military forces. As previously noted, the aura of superiority and lethality created by U.S. air operations during Desert Storm and the subsequent 12-year enforcement of the no-fly zones convinced many Iraqi officers and enlisted personnel—even before the outbreak of hostilities—that there was no way Iraqi forces could defeat a U.S. invasion. Once hostilities commenced, Coalition bombing reinforced the already-existing Iraqi calculations about the futility of resistance and further lowered

---

[40] Wong et al. (2003), p. 8.

[41] Zucchino (2003), p. 1.

[42] Moore (2003), p. A1.

[43] Zucchino (2003), p. 1. Also see Moore (2003), p. A1.

the already-faltering Iraqi troop morale. The Iraqis realized that their air defenses were inadequate to cope with fixed-wing air strikes. Indeed, no Iraqi aircraft flew in OIF. Summarizing the views of the senior Iraqi officers he interviewed, journalist William Branigin wrote:

> U.S. airpower, combined with the lack of any Iraqi air defense capability, proved devastating not only to military equipment, but to the will to fight of soldiers and officers alike.[44]

The testimony of former Iraqi commanders and other senior personnel indicate that both the prospect and reality of precision air attacks had an enormously debilitating effect on Iraqi battlefield behavior. Concerns about air attacks motivated Iraqi soldiers to stay away from their armored vehicles and artillery and, indeed, prompted massive numbers of Iraqis to abandon their equipment on the battlefield and desert home.[45]

A team of investigative reporters who interviewed eyewitnesses and Republican Guard survivors in seven areas in which Republican Guard units had been deployed, found that "relatively few" Republican Guard troops were actually killed by air attacks or in the ground fighting. The Iraqi forces "survived aerial bombardment by keeping their distance from their armor," and when U.S. ground troops approached, the Republican Guard troops generally fled:[46]

> Iraqi soldiers learned not to sleep near their vehicles and to construe any sign of a U.S. air raid—the appearance overhead of a drone, the sound of a plane or the sudden explosion of a nearby tank—as a prompt to take cover.[47]

To avoid destruction by air attack, the commander of a 150-man Republican Guard unit in Muhmudiyah reportedly even ordered his

---

[44] Branigin (2003), p. A25.

[45] See Fisk (2003).

[46] The battlefield areas surveyed by the *Time Magazine* team were Hindiyah, Hillah, Kut, Yusufiyah, Mahmudiyah, Suwayrah and Dawrah. See McCarthy (2003), pp. 38–39.

[47] McCarthy (2003), pp. 39–40.

soldiers "to leave their tanks in the market and prepare to confront U.S. forces on foot."[48]

The large number of abandoned Iraqi tanks and APCs encountered by U.S. Army and Marine forces during their march to Baghdad is one proof that the vast majority of Republican Guard troops were unwilling to stay with their armor. In many Iraqi Republican Guard and Regular Army units, the "fear of U.S. airpower was as crippling as the air strikes themselves."[49] The above-cited interviews with enlisted Iraqi EPWs showed that Coalition air attacks and artillery shelling "sometimes catalyzed surrender—though none of the soldiers interviewed had to withstand lengthy bombardment."[50]

Senior Iraqi commanders emphasized the debilitating psychological effects of the precision of U.S. air attacks. The Republican Guard I Corps Commander, Lieutenant General Majid Husayn Ali Ibrahim Al-Dulaymi, told his interviewers that

> [o]ur units were unable to execute anything due to worries induced by psychological warfare. They were fearful of modern war, pinpoint war in all climates and in all weather. . . . Even the lowest soldier knew we couldn't stop the Americans.[51]

He described the shock he felt when a series of precision air strikes obliterated a battalion of the Republican Guard Adnan Mechanized Infantry Division that was caught in the open: "The level of precision of those attacks put real fear into the soldiers of the rest of the division. The Americans were able to induce fear throughout the army by using precision air power."[52]

---

[48] McCarthy (2003), p. 40.

[49] After being hammered by B-52 bombing, the soldiers of the Iraqi 42nd Armored Brigade defending the northern stretch of the Diyala River quickly abandoned their armor. This, despite the fact that the brigade had been dispersed to reduce its vulnerability to air attack. The brigade's tanks were still warm when the advancing U.S. Marine forces captured them. See Gordon and Trainor (2006a), p. 412.

[50] Wong et al. (2003), pp. 7–8.

[51] Quoted in Woods et al. (2006), p. 125.

[52] Quoted in Woods et al. (2006), p. 125.

The Al-Nida Armored Division, considered the Republican Guard's most effective fighting force, disintegrated as a result of the threat and reality of U.S. precision bombing. According to the division's commander, Major General Abd Al-Karim Jasim Nafus al-Majid, the combination of accurate leaflet drops and precision air strikes overall had a "terrible effect" on his forces.[53] After the troops in the division's 42nd Brigade "were hit very effectively for five days" in their prepared positions, most of the troops deserted. After one particularly heavy air strike on Al-Nida's 43rd Brigade, virtually all the brigade's troops abandoned their positions and vehicles and ran away.[54]

By the time U.S. forces closed in on Baghdad, the massive desertions and equipment losses caused by the prospect and reality of U.S. air attacks had reduced the Al-Nida Division to a mere skeleton. Out of an original division complement of some 13,000 troops and more than 500 armored vehicles, less than 1,000 soldiers and 50 or so vehicles remained.[55] This, despite the fact that the Al-Nida Division never engaged U.S. forces in the ground fighting.[56]

The threat of U.S. air attacks also undermined the fighting will of some of Iraq's air defense elements. The commander of a Baghdad air defense unit, Colonel Rafed Abdul Mehdi, reported that his unit would move its missiles several times a day to avoid being bombed. However, as U.S. air attacks on targets in and around Baghdad intensified, "almost all" the soldiers who operated the missiles abandoned their launchers.[57] The threat of bombing also had pernicious effects on other Iraqi battlefield behavior, such as deterring Iraqi units from using their communications equipment for fear of inviting discovery and destruction from U.S. air attacks.

An infantryman from a 2,000-man Republican Guard unit deployed to defend the city of Kut, southeast of Baghdad, contended

---

[53] Woods et al. (2006), pp. 125–126.

[54] Woods et al. (2006), pp. 128–129.

[55] Woods et al. (2006), p. 126.

[56] Woods et al. (2006), pp. 127–128.

[57] Walt (2003).

that the nine days of bombing that preceded the actual engagement with ground forces had broken the spirit of his unit:

> From the start lots of my friends were killed by the bombs. There were at least 150 who died in the first few days. The bombs fell everywhere, blowing people apart and destroying everything . . . at any moment you thought you were going to die. I was so afraid, and so were my comrades.[58]

After three days of fighting a losing battle with U.S. ground forces, in which the unit's Russian-made T-55 and T-72 tanks that had survived the aerial bombardment proved no match for the better-armed U.S. Abrams tanks, the infantryman and "most of those around him" decided to desert rather than die for a cause already lost.[59]

As a Republican Guard general observed, desertions were to be expected in a war in which defeat and death were inevitable: "Even in the Republican Guard, the men were left with no choice—either they left their posts or they died."[60]

A member of the Regular Army's general staff, Colonel Ghassan, attributed the Iraqi defeat primarily to the inability of Iraqi commanders to safely move their equipment and troops because of the devastating U.S. airpower and to the disruption of communications between the commanders. Colonel Ghassan reported that the three Republican Guard divisions that Qusay Hussein had ordered repositioned to oppose the Coalition advance were essentially destroyed by U.S. air attacks when they were still about 30 miles from their designated new deployment areas south of Baghdad. "This affected the morale of the troops," Colonel Ghassan said. "The Iraqi will to fight was broken outside Baghdad."[61]

Coalition air attacks also took a heavy toll on elements of the 2nd Infantry Division that were ordered on March 25 to redeploy

---

[58] MacKinnon (2003).

[59] MacKinnon (2003).

[60] Walt (2003).

[61] Branigin (2003), p. A25.

from their bivouac area near Kifri, in northern Iraq, to the northeastern outskirts of Baghdad. The 4,000-man unit suffered few casualties from Coalition air strikes while on the march, because it moved under cover of a large dust storm that blanketed the area. However, once the unit dug in near Baghdad, it was subjected to devastating "massive air attacks." According to Major Jaburi, a Tikriti who served as a battalion commander in the 2nd Division, the 4,000-man unit lost no less than 1,400 men to Coalition air attacks between April 1 and 8.[62]

Major Jaburi claimed that the survivors nevertheless "stood their ground, and repelled" an attack by U.S. Marines on the afternoon of April 7th. Major Jaburi testified to the importance of U.S. air supremacy: "We knew that they [the U.S. Marines] were afraid to face us, but the fact they had close air support encouraged them to engage us. . . . If we had had air cover or missiles, I don't think the Americans would have dared enter Iraq, let alone Baghdad."[63]

When divisional headquarters in Baghdad ordered the unit to return to its base in the north, over one-half of the remaining men stripped off their uniforms and headed home to protect their families. At that point, Major Jaburi's own career-officer's sense of discipline was overruled by his instincts for survival: "We were shocked" that Baghdad had fallen so quickly. "The battle was over. We didn't know what to do[,] and you can't judge whether it was right or wrong." Soon Major Jaburi's commander "expressed his deepest sympathy and condolences, and said we should go home."[64]

Iraqi troops were disheartened by the ability of U.S. aircraft to find and destroy targets that the Iraqis believed were effectively camouflaged. A Republican Guard captain, Omar Khalidi, recounted his dismay when U.S. aircraft destroyed his surface-to-surface-missile unit a few nights before U.S. troops seized Baghdad. "We were surprised when they [U.S. pilots] discovered this place," said Captain Khalidi. The attack occurred late at night, during a strong sandstorm, and the

---

[62] Peterson and Ford (2003), p. 12.

[63] Peterson and Ford (2003), p. 12.

[64] Peterson and Ford (2003), p. 12.

vehicles were hidden under trees that the troops thought would mask them from observation. Two large bombs and a load of cluster munitions hit the targets, killing six members of Captain Khalidi's unit and destroying most of their equipment.[65]

"This," according to Captain Khalidi, "affected the morale of the soldiers, because they were hiding and thought nobody could find them. Some soldiers left their positions and ran away. When the big bombs hit their target, some of the vehicles just melted. And the effect of the cluster bombs was even greater, because they covered a larger area."

Reflecting the extent to which some senior Iraqi commanders had failed to grasp the technological prowess of U.S. forces, Captain Khalidi reported that most of his commanders "were sure that [his missile unit's position had been discovered] through spies, because it was impossible to find [it] through satellite or aircraft. Even if you drove by it, you couldn't find it."[66]

Coalition bombing engendered fears in the Iraqi forces about their personal survival and the safety of their families. Colonel A. T. Said, who commanded a 150-man Republican Guard unit that was deployed on March 19 to guard a bridge north of Baghdad, described the process of desertion that eventually dissolved his unit: On the day of their deployment, and without a shot having been fired, the security officer responsible for ensuring the unit's loyalty to Saddam, deserted—opening the way for others to quit. Thereafter, groups of five or six deserted every day. Once heavy Coalition air strikes began, the desertion rate accelerated.

Colonel Said reported that he raised no objection to these desertions, because he wanted to spare the lives of his teenage troops:

A soldier would say to me, "Sir, excuse me, but I cannot stay here because of the bombing. I fear for my family. I'm sorry sir." I

---

[65] Branigin (2003), p. A25.

[66] Branigin (2003), p. A25.

would say, "Don't worry. God go with you. I will be joining you soon."[67]

By the time Colonel Said's unit was ordered to withdraw into Baghdad on April 5 to guard a strategic site, only five of his soldiers remained. All the others had quit, including his commanding officer, General Mahmoud al-Ani. Lacking orders, and threatened by American tank forces, Colonel Said and his remaining troops discarded their uniforms and headed for home, no one having died in combat or having fired a shot in the defense of Baghdad.[68]

Even in Iraq's northern areas, where there was no threat from significant U.S. ground forces, air strikes caused massive desertions. An Iraqi general, for example, revealed that the Iraqi 5th Infantry division's defenses around Mosul collapsed after only "two days of bombing."[69]

A Regular Army division suffered air attacks and huge desertions when it attempted to move from its deployment area near Mosul to Baghdad to meet the Coalition offensive. The division commander, General Jalal Muhammad, reported that, of the 7,800 troops he had when the division started its redeployment, only 50 remained by the time it reached the capital. General Muhammad attributes his division's evaporation to Coalition's air attacks, which his troops were helpless to counter:

> We were bombed before we even left our base—while we were packing. The rest fled or died along the way. My soldiers were not cowards, but it was like we were holding a stick in our hands and the enemy had an AK-47.[70]

---

[67] Blair (2003a).

[68] Blair (2003a).

[69] Woods, et al. (2006), pp. 82–83.

[70] Welsh (2004).

Why the Fedayeen Saddam, Ba'athist Militia, and Foreign Jihadists Were Motivated to Fight

In an Iraqi force structure that showed little will to fight, irregular militia forces—the Fedayeen Saddam militia, the Ba'ath Party militia, and the foreign jihadist fighters provided some of the most aggressive opposition that Coalition troops encountered. These militias and jihadists were motivated to fight either because they had a major personal stake in the survival of Saddam's regime or because they believed in the cause of defending Iraq against U.S. and other foreign invaders.

However, despite their zeal to close with Coalition forces, the battlefield effectiveness of these irregulars was limited because they were lightly armed and poorly trained and led. As a consequence, they died in large numbers.

The Fedayeen Saddam

The Fedayeen Saddam (Saddam's "Men of Sacrifice") were largely uneducated youths drawn from Saddam's al-Bu-Nasir tribe or from other clans immediately north of Baghdad, where Saddam's support was strongest. They were fanatically loyal to Saddam, having been conditioned by his cult of personality and instilled with the belief that their fate was directly tied to the fate of his regime and person.[71] The Fedayeen Saddam was organized in 1991, in part to help counter any possible future uprisings in Iraq, such as those that occurred among the Shias and Kurds following the Persian Gulf War. The Fedayeen militia was commanded by Saddam's son Uday, and probably numbered somewhere between 20,000 and 40,000 fighters.[72]

---

[71] See Kanan Makiya, "The Fedayeen Saddam Keep Shia Intifada in Check," New Perspectives Quarterly, Vol. 21, No. 3, Summer 2004, and David Blair, "Why the Fedayeen Fight for Their Lives," Telegraph (UK), March 25, 2003b.

[72] Estimates of the number of Fedayeen Saddam vary. Secretary of Defense Donald Rumsfeld estimated their probable size at "somewhere between 5,000 and 20,000," whereas Iraqi opposition sources claimed they numbered closer to 50,000. A Council of Foreign Relations estimate put the number at between 30,000 and 40,000, the latter number coinciding with the Jane's estimate of 40,000. See Makiya (2004); Blair (2003b); Council on Foreign Relations, "Iraq: What Is the Fedayeen Saddam?" updated March 31, 2003 (online at http://www.cfr.org/publication/7698/iraq.html

Members of the Fedayeen Saddam militia, who were widely hated by ordinary Iraqis, may have feared that if Saddam's regime fell they could be the subjects of severe reprisals.[73] Many Iraqi Regular Army and Republican Guard leaders found the Fedayeen Saddam's arrogant and freewheeling behavior to be repugnant, and they considered the militia members to be no more than "lower class" mercenaries. The Fedayeen were also resented because they were the recipients of special privileges: Their pay was 40 percent higher than that of the regular military, and their cars and housing were often subsidized.[74]

Among other duties, the Fedayeen acted as enforcers for the regime: suppressing anti-regime activities, policing curfews, conducting extra-judicial executions, and arresting and punishing deserters from Regular Army and Republican Guard units. Uday is also said to have used the force for "personal ends[,] placing it in charge of smuggling and using it to attack, torture and murder opponents."[75]

During the 2003 war, the Fedayeen Saddam were deployed in Iraq's urban areas. Their main functions were to cause maximum casualties among the invading Coalition units, to force regular Iraqi troops and members of the civilian population to fight (in some cases, by killing those who tried to surrender), and to put down any anti-regime uprisings that might occur in the urban areas.[76]

The Fedayeen Saddam militia presented the most consistently ferocious opposition to U.S. forces, mounting numerous, sometimes near-suicidal, attacks against the American armored and logistic elements that penetrated Baghdad and other urban centers. Aside from believing their fate to be closely joined to the survival of the regime, the

---

[as of June 14, 2007]); and "Security and Foreign Forces, Iraq," *Jane's Defence Weekly,* January 29, 2002 (online at http://www4.janes.com/K2/docprint.jsp?K2DocKey=/content1/janesdata/mags/jdw/history [as of February 5, 2003]).

[73] See Makiya (2004) and Blair (2003b).

[74] See Blair (2003b).

[75] Council on Foreign Relations (2003).

[76] See Makiya (2004) and "Iraqi Militia Defy Conventional Characterization," Associated Press, March 27, 2003 (online at http://findarticles.com/p/articles/mi_qn4196/is_20030328/ai_n10866469 [as of June 26, 2007]).

Fedayeen Saddam fighters were probably motivated to fight ferociously by the severe sanctions that awaited those militiamen who proved less than resolute or successful in battle.[77]

The Ba'ath Party Militia

Elements of the Ba'ath Party militia also fought. These Ba'ath Party fighters—who probably numbered in the thousands—were apparently drawn in part from the 40,000 or so "full" members of the party who were particularly loyal to Saddam Hussein. As members of Iraq's ruling elite, they also had an important stake in the survival of the regime.[78]

In the run-up to the war, large numbers of Ba'ath Party members were armed and organized for combat. Aside from taking an active part in the urban fighting, the Ba'ath Party militias were also charged with preventing civilian uprisings and otherwise controlling the Iraqi public in their areas. Party loyalists were deployed in every neighborhood and, in some cities, on every block to keep civilian populations in line.[79]

Party militia members also acted to stiffen the resistance of the Iraqi regular military forces. During the British siege of Basra, Ba'ath Party militias were credited with maintaining the Iraqi resistance. The militia prevented the flight of civilians from Basra and reportedly pressured remnants of the Regular Army's 51st Division to continue fighting by threatening, in some instances, to execute the families of soldiers.[80]

---

[77] According to Fedayeen Saddam regulations, commanders were to be executed if a certain portion of their units were "defeated." Fedayeen Saddam fighters, including commanders, were also to be executed if they hesitated in carrying out their duties, cooperated with the enemy, or gave up their weapons. See Woods et al. (2006), p. 55.

[78] Some 2 million Iraqis may have been affiliated with the Ba'ath Party in one of five different membership categories: "supporter," "sympathizer," "nominee," "trainee," and "full." Candidates had to pass through the other four steps before becoming a full member. See "Baath Party Entrenched in Saddam's Cult of Personality" (2003).

[79] "Baath Party Entrenched in Saddam's Cult of Personality" (2003).

[80] "UK Troops 'Target Ba'ath Militia,'" CNN.com./World. Online at http://edition.cnn.com/2003/WORLD/meast/03/27/sprj.irq.iraq.basra/ (as of June 26, 2007).

The Foreign Jihadists

The foreign jihadists were highly motivated combatants in that they had come to Iraq for the express purpose of fighting any invading forces. As many as 5,000 to 7,000 foreign jihadists entered Iraq in the months shortly before the outbreak of hostilities and during the March and early-April fighting.[81] Most came from Syria, Jordan, and Egypt, but there were also volunteers from Saudi Arabia, Lebanon, the Palestinian territories, Algeria, Libya, the United Arab Emirates, and Afghanistan.[82] Many of the Syrian volunteers had "close tribal and cultural links to Iraqis across the border" and "felt it their duty to fight."[83] The numbers of Syrian jihadists alone is reliably reported to have been in the thousands.[84] Many Palestinians living in Jordan were also recruited before the war to fight in Iraq.[85] Upon arrival in Iraq, they were pro-

---

[81] This was not the first time foreign fighters had entered Iraq. Between 1998 and summer 2002, some thousands of other "Arab volunteers" had received training in Fedayeen Saddam paramilitary camps. Most of these volunteers returned home upon the completion of their training. See Woods et al. (2006), p. 54. Also see Stephen F. Hayes, "Saddam's Terror Camps," *The Weekly Standard*, January 16, 2006. Online at http://www.weeklystandard. com/Utilities/printer_preview.asp?idArticle=6550&R=EB3D2AC08.

[82] While Arab governments found it politically difficult to prevent their citizens from joining the jihad in Iraq, some tried to hamper the process. Egypt, for example, after the start of OIF, "found itself faced with thousands of Egyptians demanding an opportunity to join their Arab brothers to drive off the Coalition 'unbelievers.'" The government assured the would-be jihadists that nothing would stand in their way, in that "Combating injustice is a religious duty. . . ." But in reality, the government "buried their attempts to fight in the red tape of Egypt's formidable bureaucracy" (Andrew McGregor, "Al-Azhar, Egyptian Islam and the War in Iraq," *Terrorism Monitor* [The Jamestown Foundation], Vol. 2 Issue 12, June 17, 2004. Online at http://www.jamestown.org/publications_details [as of June 22, 2004]).

[83] See Ahmed Hashim, "Foreign Involvement in the Iraqi Insurgency," *Terrorism Monitor* [The Jamestown Foundation], Vol. 2, Issue 16, August 12, 2004. Online at http://www. jamestown.org/print_friendly.php?volume_id=400&issue_id=3047&article_id=2368398.

[84] According to former Syrian Vice President Abdel Halim Khaddam, "some thousands" of Syrians entered "Iraq for jihad" during the war. Khaddam, who was a key architect of Syria's Iraq policy before breaking with the regime, claims that those Syrians eventually "came back," as they had been "deceived by the bad treatment they received from the people of Saddam Hussein" (Christopher Dickey, "'Mafia State,'" *Newsweek*, January 5, 2006. Online at http://www.msnbc.msn.com/id/10728635/site/newsweek/print/1/displaymode/1098/ [as of September 6, 2006]).

[85] Hashim (2004), p. 1 and n. 2.

vided light weapons and were given weapons training at a variety of camps, sometimes in the company of Fedayeen Saddam and Al Quds personnel.[86] Those foreign jihadists with previous military service were sent to a training camp for the "experienced." A Palestinian, who had served in the Jordanian Army, reported attending one such training camp with 500 to 700 other militarily experienced jihadists.[87]

According to Arab media interviews with the foreign fighters, their experience in Iraq was, in some cases, not a happy one. Some found the training they received to be "poor and disorganized," their logistics support to be inadequate, and nearly half their weaponry to be nonoperable. They also had not anticipated the intensity of the Coalition's firepower and found it fruitless to attempt "to fight off the invaders with [their] light weapons."[88] But many were nevertheless, prepared to fight on to the end.[89] Indeed, Syrian jihadists were credited with the hardest fighting in some battlefield areas. U.S. Marines reportedly encountered heavy resistance from Syrian jihadists near the town of Kut. Similarly, an estimated 200 to 300 Syrian jihadists, organized into 20- to 30-man platoons, mounted most of the attacks against American troops at Objective Curley in Baghdad.[90]

They also found their Iraqi allies to be wanting. One jihadist was shocked by the sense of panic that seemed to pervade the Iraqi troops: "The Iraqi soldiers were scared to death, with some even fainting."[91] Some of the Arab fighters complained of being placed in overly exposed positions by their Iraqi officers and of being fired upon by Iraqi troops. The jihadists who were stationed in Baghdad reported that they were

---

[86] See Steven Stalinsky, *Arab and Muslim Jihad Fighters in Iraq*, Washington, D.C.: Middle East Media and Research Institute (MEMRI), Special Report No. 19, July 27, 2003. Online at http://www.memri.org/bin/opener.cgi?Page=archives&ID=SR1903 (as of May 4, 2005).

[87] Another Palestinian jihadist reported being trained with a "couple of hundred" other Arab volunteers and members of the Al Quds and Fedayeen Saddam militias in the Al-Sadeer district of Baghdad. See Stalinsky (2003).

[88] Stalinsky (2003).

[89] Some of the jihadists fully expected to be "martyred" (killed) in Iraq. Stalinsky (2003).

[90] See Gordon and Trainor (2006a), pp. 336, 408, 418, and 431.

[91] Stalinsky (2003).

suddenly abandoned with no warning by their Iraqi commanders and cohorts on April 8, and that thereafter they were shunned by a hostile Iraqi civilian populace.[92]

Many of the Paramilitaries Also Deserted

Not all the paramilitaries fought to the bitter end. There were reports of significant Fedayeen Saddam and Ba'athist militia desertions in Nasiriyah, Najaf, and other southern Iraqi cities. By March 31st, desertions among Ba'athist and Al Quds militiamen, for example, had reduced the total number of defenders in the Central Euphrates region city of As-Samawah to only about 200 men. Ba'ath Party officials, who were responsible for the defense of the city, complained that "they no longer had any men."[93] Massive desertions had occurred even before U.S. forces had entered As-Samawah.

In Baghdad, after some intense fights with U.S. Army and Marine forces, the paramilitaries simply faded away. On the day before Baghdad's fall,

> [f]rom dusk to dawn, Baghdad's defenses virtually disintegrated. Thousands of Ba'ath Party militiamen, who had manned every street corner, bridge and intersection, changed into street clothes and went home. Saddam's Fedayeen, black-clad militiamen, who had vowed to fight to the death, were gone by morning, some of them leaving their weapons behind.[94]

The desertions typically followed the disappearance of the officers commanding the paramilitary forces. Some Ba'ath Party militia commanders were said to have abandoned their troops on the pretext that

---

[92] See Stalinsky (2003) and McGregor (2004).

[93] The Al Quds officials also reported "that they no longer had any soldiers." When the local Ba'ath Party leaders in As-Samawah decamped on April 3rd, civic order in the city quickly disintegrated and "mobs started looting everything." See statements by Lieutenant General Yahya Taha Huwaysh-Fadani Al-Ani, assistant military adviser to the Ba'ath commander in the Central Euphrates region, quoted in Woods et al. (2006), p. 136.

[94] Anthony Shadid, "For Iraq's Leaders and Loyalists, a Vanishing Act," *The Washington Post*, April 12, 2003b, p. A21.

"they were leaving for dinner." One senior Ba'ath Party official claimed that he was told by his supervisor to abandon his post on April 7 and return home because the militia's "rifles and rocket-propelled grenades were no match for the might of American forces."[95]

One Ba'ath Party militiaman stated that he, like others, had never bargained for a fight with an army. He reported that when the Americans first entered Baghdad, senior Ba'ath Party leaders

> threatened him and others with a gun to make sure they would fight. But it was the leadership's desertion on the morning of the city's fall that ended any pretense of defending Baghdad in what virtually everyone considered a doomed fight.[96]

The Effects of PSYOPS

The Coalition mounted a major PSYOPS campaign in Iraq both before and during OIF. Some 19 million leaflets were dropped on Iraqi territory between October 2002 and when the ground combat began on March 20, 2003. An additional 31 million leaflets were dropped during the fighting that followed. Thousands of hours of radio broadcasts were also directed at Iraqi audiences, from both land stations and Hercules C-130 Commando Solo aircraft. To cue the potential radio listeners, leaflets were dropped instructing the Iraqis about the frequencies over which the Coalition's "Information Radio" could be heard.[97]

Many leaflets were directed at the Iraqi civilian population, telling the public that the Coalition's purpose was not to hurt them but to free them from Saddam's oppression. These leaflets also asked the public to cooperate with the Coalition and to remain out of harm's way.[98]

---

[95] Shadid (2003b), p. A21.

[96] Shadid (2003b), p. A21.

[97] A description of the various leaflets dropped in OIF is provided by Herbert A. Friedman, *Operation Iraqi Freedom*. Online at http://www.psywarrior.com/OpnIraqiFreedom.html (as of July 10, 2003).

[98] Leaflet messages intended for civilian audiences attempted to reassure the Iraqi public that the Coalition's only purpose in coming to Iraq was to "put an end to the oppression

Leaflets intended for Saddam's military forces attempted to influence the Iraqi troops to (1) surrender, (2) abandon their weapons, (3) return to their families, and (4) avoid certain battlefield responses, for example, not to target Coalition aircraft or employ WMD.[99]

It is difficult to assess the effects this PSYOPS campaign had on the behavior of Iraqi forces. The surrender appeals, which were a major focus of the PSYOPS campaign, apparently had little direct effect on Iraqi troop behavior, because comparatively few Iraqi units or individuals surrendered. However, massive numbers of Iraqis did abandon their armored vehicles and crew-served weapons and returned to their homes, which suggests these particular appeals may have had some effect. As with most PSYOPS evaluations, it is difficult to differentiate between the effects of PSYOPS appeals and the psychological effects of Coalition air strikes and ground-force attacks. Interviews with Iraqi officers and troops indicate that the air strikes and ground-force attacks were the principal motivating factor. It was the dread of impending battle, the experience of actual battle, and the absence of any motivation to fight that caused the vast majority of Iraqi forces to abandon their weapons and return home.

American PSYOPS had little effect on rank-and-file troops in some areas, because of a lack of radio receivers and Iraqi security countermeasures. An Iraqi colonel, whose unit had been located in Amarah in southern Iraq near the Iranian border, reported that PSYOPS radio broadcasts warning Iraqi soldiers not to fight and instructing them on how to surrender were rarely heard, since few troops owned radios.

---

caused by Saddam and his regime." The leaflets further announced the Coalition's desire not to harm the Iraqi people and directed civilians to keep away from military targets, stay in their homes, and not interfere with Coalition forces. See leaflets IZD=022a, IZD-024, and IZD-1000 (Friedman, 2003).

[99] Examples of Coalition messages: (1) calling on troops to surrender were leaflets IZD-0330, IZD-033p, IZD-069, and IZD-8104; (2) calling on troops to abandon their weapons were leaflets IZD-017e and IZD-017d; (3) calling on troops to return to their families were leaflets IZD-029, IZD-050, and IZD-7509; and (4) calling on troops to avoid certain actions were leaflets IZD-041 and IZD-2502 (Friedman, 2003).

Similarly, the colonel reported that his troops had had little exposure to PSYOPS leaflets because Iraqi military intelligence and Mukhabarat internal security agents scooped them up first: "The soldiers would see them fall, but were not allowed to read them. . . . The Army has lots of Baath infiltrators, which kept a tight grip and collected those very fast."[100]

While the message content of the leaflets did not incite desertions, other Iraqi officers suggested that the fall of leaflets on their locations intimidated Iraqi soldiers, who realized that U.S. bombers could have just as easily dropped bombs on their positions.[101]

The Al-Nida Division Commander reported that the accurate drops of Coalition leaflets helped to undermine the fighting will of his units. Because the accuracy of the leaflet drops convinced the soldiers that the American pilots knew their exact location, the Al-Nida troops felt as though they were targeted in "a sniper's sight." The ability of U.S. aircraft to fly over their positions with virtual immunity underscored the regime's impotence. The devastation caused by precision air strikes on exposed positions greatly magnified these demoralization effects.[102] As the Al-Nida Commander described the troop reaction,

[t]he air attacks were [the] most effective message. The soldiers who did see the leaflets and then saw the air attacks knew the leaflets were true. They believed the message after that, if they were still alive. Overall they had a terrible effect on us.[103]

---

[100] Peterson and Ford (2003), p. 12.

[101] Thom Shanker, "Regime Thought War Unlikely, Iraqis Tell U.S.," *The New York Times*, February 12, 2004.

[102] Woods et al. (2006), p. 125.

[103] Quoted in Woods et al. (2006), p. 126. Also see Gordon and Trainor (2006a), p. 373, citing Woods et al.

Iraqi views on the effectiveness of the U.S. information operations to persuade senior Iraqi officers and officials to desert or join with the United States were mixed.[104]

One former Iraqi colonel believed that the PSYOPS messages directed at senior commanders via fax and emails had a "big impact" before those lines of communication were cut 10 days before the start of the war:

> Of course it has an impact—if one commander receives a fax and gives it to his senior, in this simple way the officer knows of the U.S. technical superiority. . . . Imagine him thinking: "If the Americans are able to get into the mind of a senior commander this way, how can I protect a whole division?"[105]

Interrogations of other Iraqi officers suggest that the disruptive effects of such contacts were indirect. When calls went out to the private telephone numbers of selected senior officials in Iraq asking them to turn against Saddam Hussein and avoid war, the Arabic speakers "making the calls were so fluent that the recipients did not believe the calls were from Americans."

Instead, the Iraqi officials believed the calls were part of a "loyalty test" mounted by Saddam's security services. "Afraid of arrest, incarceration, torture and even death, they refused to cooperate." But as a consequence, the officials limited their own calls or stopped using the telephone altogether, which hampered "their ability to communicate in the critical days before the war."[106]

---

[104]For discussions of the operations to forge alliances with Iraqi officers before and during OIF, see Douglas Jehl, with Dexter Filkins, "U.S. Moved to Undermine Iraqi Military Before War," *The New York Times*, August 10, 2003, p. A1; Rowan Scarborough, "U.S. Seeks Surrender of Iraqi Leaders," *The Washington Times*, March 17, 2003, p. A10, and Peter Baker, "U.S. to Negotiate Capitulation Agreements with Iraqi Military, *The Washington Post*, March 17, 2003 (online at http://www-tech.mit.edu/V123/N13/iraq-military.13w.html [as of June 14, 2007]). The very surfacing of such operations in the media had a psychological effect on Saddam and senior Iraqi leaders, because it increased distrust in the Iraqi officer ranks.

[105]Peterson and Ford (2003), p. 12.

[106]Shanker (2004).

The U.S.-Arabic speakers who broadcasted PSYOPS messages on the Iraqi's own military communications nets, although detectable as non-Iraqis, nevertheless had a major effect on at least some Iraqi audiences. The brigadier general who commanded Baghdad's missile air defenses reports that the voices that cut into his military radio traffic signaled Iraq's coming defeat:

> I would talk to my missile crews and suddenly the Americans would come on the same frequency. . . . They would talk in Arabic—with Egyptian and Lebanese accents—and they would say, "We have taken Nasiriyah, we have captured Najaf, we are at Baghdad airport." It was the psychological war that did the worst damage to us. The Americans knew all our frequencies. By then, we had no radio news broadcast of our own, just the Americans talking directly to us on our radio net. I could have replied directly to those voices, but we were ordered not to, and I obeyed my own security.[107]

Summing up the effects of these intrusions, the general stated,

> I think it was the psychological war that won over the 'real' war for us. Those Americans talking to us over our own radios—that was what succeeded. We could no longer talk to each other on the radios. But we could hear the Americans.[108]

The Effects of the Capture of Baghdad

The arrival of U.S. forces on the outskirts of Baghdad surprised many Iraqi senior officers and had a devastating effect on morale. The subsequent U.S "Thunder Run" armor attacks into Baghdad and the sudden evacuation of the city by Saddam Hussein and other top Iraqi leaders essentially put an end to organized resistance within the country.

---

[107] Fisk (2003).

[108] Fisk (2003).

Desertions soared as U.S. forces neared Baghdad. Major Jaffer Sadiq, a Special Forces commander, reported that after being ordered on April 2 to rush to Baghdad from the northern city of Kirkuk, he was told that he would be joining some 4,000 Republican Guard troops defending a site in the capital. However, when he arrived in Baghdad, he found fewer than 1,000 Republican Guard troops and "most of these" deserted by the time the first U.S. "Thunder Run" had been made through southwest Baghdad on April 5.

Major Sadiq reports that, between April 2 and April 5, desertions had depleted his company, from 131 men to 10:

> I woke up on the morning of April 5 and an entire battalion was gone. They had become vapors.[109]

Colonel Abdul Kareem Abdul Razzaq, the commander of a 1,500-man Regular Army unit charged with protecting a major highway interchange on the edge of Baghdad, described how the morale and behavior of his troops changed with the approach of American forces. As was the case with many Iraqi officers and enlisted personnel in the Baghdad area, news reports by the Iraqi media and "Baghdad Bob" (Mohammed Said al-Sahaf, the Iraqi Minister of Information) about the strong Iraqi resistance in Nasiriyah and Basra during the first days of fighting "heartened his men":[110]

> All the news was very good. We were stopping the American forces. Spirits were high among the soldiers in Baghdad. They were motivated to defend the city.[111]

However, soon after American forces fought their way into the Baghdad International Airport, the men began to desert. About half of Colonel Razzaq's remaining men deserted; the other half hid in build-

---

[109] Zucchino (2003), p. 1.

[110] Moore (2003), p. A1. Other Iraqi officers also report that morale rose after TV pictures and other media depicted the American prisoners captured in Nasiriyah and the continued Iraqi resistance in that city. See Branigin (2003), p. A25.

[111] Moore (2003), p. A1.

ings lining the airport road. On April 7, he received a final command to continue fighting. He replied: "Yes, we'll do it. [But] we weren't convinced. We didn't do it." Colonel Razzaq then collected his men and allowed them to decide. "Everyone went home."[112]

The fact that U.S. units had reached Baghdad undermined the fighting will of Iraqi units elsewhere in the country. A Regular Army unit based in Amarah in southern Iraq also began to disintegrate on April 3rd, when news was heard that American forces had reached Baghdad. Troops began to desert when the unit's food supply was cut off the next day. As an Iraqi colonel stationed with the unit described the situation, "Soldiers started asking: 'Why are we using the reserve food?' and on April 4 they began to run away."[113]

When word came that American forces had entered the capital, senior Iraqi officers were "stunned." An Iraqi Air Force brigadier general described the reaction at his Baghdad headquarters:

> When we were working in my operations room and we heard that the Americans had arrived in the city, none of us there believed it. This was impossible, we thought.[114]

A Republican Guard colonel encountered a similar reaction after he returned to his headquarters an hour northeast of Baghdad and informed his fellow commanders that U.S. tanks had penetrated Baghdad: The other officers "called him a liar."[115]

Some officers continued to be deluded by the optimistic reports of the Iraqi Minister of Information, who brazenly claimed that the Baghdad International Airport had been retaken by Iraqi troops.[116] Republican Guard Captain Omar Khalidi reports that his unit's spirits soared

---

[112] Moore (2003), p. A1.

[113] Peterson and Ford (2003), p. 12.

[114] See Fisk (2003).

[115] See Zucchino (2003), p. 1.

[116] According to the Iraqi report, the counterattack had killed 400 U.S. soldiers, captured 200 prisoners, and destroyed 80 U.S. tanks and other fighting vehicles. See Branigin (2003), p. A25.

at the news of the "glorious victory" at the airport, only to be dashed almost immediately again when the U.S. 3rd Infantry Division's 2nd Brigade staged its first "Thunder Run" through southern Baghdad:

> It was as if that last battle had no effect. . . . It was a very big shock. Everyone was surprised that a military force could pass through all the Republican Guard and Special Republican Guard forces surrounding the [presidential palaces], and everyone became afraid. [With the forays into the capitol came] unimaginably heavy bombing. . . . After it was all over, we knew [the airport counterattack report] was an exaggeration.[117]

Iraqi general officers also believed the story of an Iraqi victory at the airport. A Republican Guard General, Mohammed Daash, was dispatched to check out the rumor that four or five U.S. tanks had survived the Iraqi counterattack. General Daash reportedly returned to his headquarters in a state of panic. "Four or five tanks!" he exclaimed to his fellow generals. "Are you out of your minds? The whole damn American Army is at the airport!"[118]

By April 7, according to eyewitnesses, Saddam and Qusay had been reduced to attempting to command the remaining Iraqi forces from a roving convoy of four-wheel-drive Toyotas that was trying to stay one step ahead of the U.S. tanks operating in Baghdad at that moment.[119] A Republican Guard division commander said he met with Saddam and Qusay at the 14th of July Bridge in central Bagh-

---

[117] Branigin (2003), p. A25.

[118] Zucchino (2003), p. 1.

[119] Saddam had apparently realized that defeat was close at hand by April 6. In a meeting with senior Iraqi leaders on that date, Saddam exhibited a tone that Tariq Aziz construed to be "that of a man 'who had lost his will to resist' and 'knew the regime was coming to an end.'" At a meeting with his inner circle on April 7, Saddam conceded "'that the army divisions were no longer capable of defending Baghdad and that he would have a meeting with the Ba'ath Regional Commanders to enlist them in the final defense of the regime.'" At a later meeting on the same day, Saddam ordered that Baghdad be divided into four quadrants, each commanded by "loyal Ba'ath stalwarts" who were to defend Baghdad to their deaths. However, his plan for such a last-ditch defense was never executed. See Woods et al. (2006), p. 149.

dad the morning of April 7. According to the general, Saddam and Qusay were aware at that point that the Special Republican Guard and Republican Guard troops assigned to protect the main palace complex had deserted. When informed that an American armored column was advancing toward Baghdad's strategic Jumhuriya Bridge, Saddam ordered 12 pickup trucks of Fedayeen Saddam to the bridge to repel the column. "Imagine," said the general, "a few pickup trucks against two battalions" of U.S. tanks and Bradley fighting vehicles.[120]

Another eyewitness, Harith Ahmed Uraibi, an archivist at the Republican presidential palace and a Ba'ath Party militiaman, also stumbled upon Saddam's convoy in front of a restaurant near the Jumhuriya Bridge, after Uraibi had fled the palace on foot when U.S. tanks overran it on April 7. Saddam shouted at him: "What's going on at the palaces?" Uraibi said: "I told him, 'Mr. President, everything is finished,' He didn't say anything. His convoy just took off across the bridge, away from the palaces and all the tanks."[121]

Over the next two days, Saddam continued to evade capture, moving from one safe house to another. His remaining regular military forces, Ba'ath Party and Fedayeen Saddam militiamen, and their various commanders evaporated. By the time Saddam abandoned the city in a white Oldsmobile heading north on the morning of April 10, there no longer was anything in Baghdad for him to command.[122] As Captain Khalidi, the Republican Guard officer, summarized it:

> In the end, when [U.S. troops] entered Baghdad, everything was messed up. . . . There were no orders. We didn't know where the commanders went. We didn't know what to do. So everyone just went home.[123]

---

[120] The Republican Guard general who reported on the meeting answered questions relayed by an aide and refused to allow his name to be used because he feared he would be arrested by U.S. occupation forces. See Zucchino (2003), p. 1.

[121] Zucchino (2003), p. 1.

[122] Accounts of Saddam's last days in Baghdad are provided by his and his son Uday's bodyguards. See "Treachery: How Iraq Went to War Against Saddam" (2004) and Philp (2003).

[123] Branigin (2003), p. A25.

CHAPTER SIX

Superior Military Capabilities Gave Coalition Forces an Overwhelming Advantage

The Coalition's domination of the battlefield in OIF was also due to its capability to deploy highly trained and motivated fighting forces, gain air supremacy, find targets and strike them promptly with accurate aerial and ground firepower, and advance ground forces rapidly and sustain them over long distances. The Coalition's objective of securing a prompt, low-casualty takedown of Saddam's regime was also facilitated by a battle plan that identified Baghdad as the Iraqi regime's center of gravity and that provided for a scheme of maneuver that would allow U.S. forces to seize the capital rapidly.[1]

Iraqi Forces Could Not Withstand the Weight and Accuracy of Coalition Firepower

In almost every aspect of the fighting, Coalition forces demonstrated a marked superiority over their Iraqi opponents. The discrepancy in capability was most telling in the ability of the Coalition's ground and air forces to deliver accurate, lethal fire on Iraqi targets.

In some instances, the weight of the U.S. firepower caused the Iraqi defenders to melt away. Iraqi Regular Army Lieutenant Colonel Mahmood Sharhan described his reaction to the Marine bombardment he experienced near the Diyala River at the eastern boundary of Baghdad:

---

[1] See Fontenot, Degen, and Tohn (2004), pp. 45–52.

It was every man for himself. You just had to make your own decisions. The bombardment was so heavy, and it made no attempt to distinguish between civilian and military areas.[2]

Colonel Sharhan abandoned his position on the morning of April 6, an act that was replicated elsewhere in his brigade, even by those who had vowed to fight. He recounted how a tank commander in his brigade had told Saddam that "he wanted to change the name of his unit to the Al-Samood, 'the unit which struggles.'" In the end, the tank commander "didn't fire a single shot at the Americans[,] and all the tanks were captured."[3]

The accurate and withering firepower of U.S. air and ground forces took a huge toll on those Iraqi soldiers and militiamen who attempted to resist. Mohamed Shebab, a Fedayeen Saddam fighter who participated in the vicious hour-and-a-half firefight with U.S. forces at the international airport, described the one-sided nature of that battle:

> The fighting was fierce. They had planes and tanks, and all we had were machine guns, rocket-propelled grenades and hand grenades. . . . We had to withdraw. We just couldn't stand up to them. There were only about 25 of us left. Most of the Fedayeen were killed.[4]

On occasion, the availability of close air support (CAS) allowed numerically inferior U.S. and allied forces at the immediate point of attack to defeat larger Iraqi units. Once the outnumbered U.S. Special Operations Forces and Kurdish Peshmerga militia fighters in northern Iraq began to receive air support, they began to make gains against Iraqi divisions defending along the Green line. Air support was also critical to the success of Operation Viking Hammer—the mission to destroy the Ansar al-Islam terrorist base in northern Iraq.[5]

---

[2] Frontline Transcript (2003), p. 29.

[3] Frontline Transcript (2003), pp. 35–36.

[4] Frontline Transcript (2003), pp. 23–24.

[5] See Murray and Scales (2003), pp. 190–193.

When Iraqi forces threatened to overrun the U.S. unit holding the newly captured bridge at Objective Monty on the northern out-skirts of Baghdad on April 6 and 7, the U.S. unit's commander called for his "supporting artillery to fire his final protective fire (FPF)" along a previously designated line just outside his position.[6] The resulting combination of continuous rapid U.S. artillery fire, close air support strikes, and direct fires "stopped the enemy cold."[7]

The plans of some Republican Guard commanders to keep their armor dispersed—to make it more difficult for U.S. aircraft to destroy it efficiently—and then to regroup the armor at the last moment to face U.S. ground forces, never could be executed. The Iraqi armor was mostly destroyed or abandoned before U.S. tanks arrived. According to a colonel who spent 21 years in the Republican Guard, the Iraqi com-mand's plan to bog down U.S. forces in ground fighting was doomed from the outset. As the Republican Guard colonel put it:

> They forgot that we are missing air power. That was a big mistake. U.S. military technology is beyond belief.[8]

The Coalition Could Attack Iraqi Forces at Standoff Distances and at Night

The Iraqis mounted their largest offensive operation of the war on the night of April 3–4, in a belated attempt to destroy the U.S. forces that gained a lodgment on the eastern side of the Euphrates River near the bridge at Objective Peach. General Hamdani, the Republican Guard II Corps Commander, mounted a counterattack along three axes, using armor, artillery, and infantry elements of the 10th Armored Brigade of the Republican Guard Medina Division, the Special Forces 3rd Bri-

---

[6] Final protective fires are called for only "if the defense gets desperate." The fight at Objec-tive Monty was the only occasion when FPF was called for in OIF. See Fontenot, Degen, and Tohn (2004), pp. 375–376.

[7] Fontenot, Degen, and Tohn (2004), p. 376.

[8] McCarthy (2003), p. 40.

gade, and the Republican Guard Nebuchadnezzar Infantry Division.[9] All told, the attacking Medina armored force consisted of some 15 tanks and 30 to 40 armored personnel carriers, supported by artillery mortars.[10]

Lieutenant Colonel Ernest "Rock" Marcone, who commanded the 3rd Infantry battalion at Objective Peach, described how a tank company under his command (without the loss of a single soldier) was able to assist in the nighttime destruction of the attacking Iraqi armored formation before it could effectively engage his forces:

> . . . We could see them [at] long ranges, and we were able to engage them and destroy them very effectively. The engagement didn't last very long. We allowed them to come into the kill zone, in the engagement area. Once they got in, they couldn't get out, because behind them, artillery is falling, and behind the artillery, we had close air support coming in. The lead units were being engaged by main gun, machine gun, and 25 mm [gun]. So they were under fire—suppress[ion] immediately.
>
> The units behind them all piled up on the road, and then our artillery and CAS came in, basically raking the column. It started at [0300]. The main attack about [0400], and by [0530], they were completely destroyed. The 10th Brigade had ceased to exist.
>
> The amazing part . . . is that we didn't realize how big the force we were fighting [was], and it was one tank company that fought that brigade. He [the company commander, Captain Robbins] never called for reinforcements. I had a company on reserve that was defending the bridge itself, and was also ready to move to reinforce north to east. Captain Robbins and his men had the

---

[9] Interview with Lieutenant General Hamdani (2004).

[10] Interview with Lieutenant Colonel Ernest "Rock" Marcone, "The Invasion of Iraq: An Oral History," *Frontline*, PBS, posted March 9, 2004. Online at http://www.pbs.org/wgbh/pages/frontline/shows/invasion/interviews/marcone.html (as of February 27, 2004). Lieutenant Colonel Marcone was the battalion commander of the 69th Armored Battalion of the 3rd Infantry Division's 1st Brigade.

situation well in hand against the clearly superior force—he was one company.[11]

General Hamdani, who had fought in five previous wars and who had "joined the front lines in [the] battle" at Objective Peach, supported Colonel Marcone's account. General Hamdani claimed that his men "had high spirits and a strong will to fight" because he had told them that the "honor of Iraq and the fate of Baghdad" were at stake.[12] But this bravado was all for naught, when "a fierce battle took place":

> The enemy used enormous firepower. It looked like napalm. Rocket launchers would fire groups of rockets, about 12 rockets each, that would explode in the air, burning whatever it faces on its way with flames. . . .
>
> The battle that took place didn't look even like action movies, because events were so fast. I didn't have a single tank intact; it was either damaged or destroyed. I didn't have a single vehicle left. The battle reached a point where the army commander [myself] was fighting with a machine gun. The groups of command and communication were completely destroyed.
>
> . . . From the dawn . . . until sunset, the Air Force destroyed anything that moved. Then the Americans broke through fiercely, as if it was programmed. Anything that moved was hit by tanks, armored vehicles, Apaches, and jet fighters, whether it was civilian or military, Republican Guard or not . . . The amount of fire and destruction was beyond description.[13]

General Hamdani then attempted to salvage what was left of the Medina Division but found that "there was no solid force left." He made an abortive attempt to collect stragglers, but encountered "total

---

[11] Interview with Lieutenant Colonel Marcone (2004).

[12] As noted previously, General Hamdani later acknowledged that this belief in the strong motivation and morale of his troops was "mistaken." (Interview with Lieutenant General Hamdani, 2004.)

[13] Interview with Lieutenant General Hamdani (2004).

chaos. No officer could gather forces to do anything."[14] After hiding in a palm grove for a number of days, General Hamdani returned to his family in Baghdad.

Lamenting the fate that befell Iraq shortly after the defeat of his forces, General Hamdani voiced the sense of shame that was shared by many other senior Iraqi officers: "The situation was so tragic. I wished I was martyred a day or two days ago, so I wouldn't see this situation, because Baghdad has fallen, and we, the army commanders, did nothing to stop this historic fall."[15]

Another disadvantage Iraqi forces faced was that U.S. forces could see and kill them at night. The Iraqis lacked sufficient night-vision devices for their tanks, as well as for their troops. Moreover, the Iraqis did not understand the capabilities of American night-vision optics, particularly the capability provided by night-vision scopes wedded to laser target designators. As a consequence, Iraqi and jihadist forces were sometimes "wholly unaware that they could be observed through American night optics."[16]

Coalition Armor Dominated in the Ground Fighting

Coalition tanks and armored infantry fighting vehicles enabled Coalition ground forces to close with and destroy enemy elements with virtual immunity. Tanks almost always led the U.S. ground advance, and in meeting engagements were able to bring enemy forces under effective fire immediately. During urban fighting, U.S. armor proved particularly effective in fending off the attacks mounted by the Fedayeen Saddam militiamen and foreign jihadists. One valuable attribute of

---

[14] Interview with Lieutenant General Hamdani (2004).

[15] Interview with Lieutenant General Hamdani (2004).

[16] For accounts of the battlefield advantages night-vision optics gave an American Marine reconnaissance unit in OIF, see Evan Wright, *Generation Kill*, New York: G. P. Putnam's Sons, 2004, pp. 119, 217, 241–243, and 250.

U.S. tanks was their high resistance to enemy fire.[17] A Republican Guard soldier said he and his fellow infantrymen were dismayed when their RPGs "bounced harmlessly off the Abrams' thick armour."[18]

The Speed of U.S. Maneuvers Surprised and Demoralized the Iraqi Defenders

American commanders in OIF emphasized the importance of maintaining a fast pace in the advance of their forces. As the CFLCC, Lieutenant General McKiernan, described his "intent" from the very beginning of the invasion: "Fast is more lethal than slower. Fast is more final."[19] The combination of rapidly moving U.S. forces and poor Iraqi situational awareness, which was partly a product of that fast movement, undermined the Iraqi ability to mount a coherent defense.

V Corps Commander Lieutenant General Wallace believed that one of the reasons the Republican Guard put up so little fight was that U.S. forces had outmaneuvered them: "We got through the Karbala Gap and we got around behind them, and there's nothing more demoralizing to an army that's looking to the south [than] to have the bad guys show up on your flank and to your rear."[20]

A concrete example of such demoralization occurred on April 4, when elements of the 2nd Brigade, 3rd Infantry Division simultaneously attacked—from the rear—elements of two Republican Guard Medina Division brigades that were dispersed in palm groves and towns along Routes 1 and 8, south of Baghdad. Colonel David Perkins, the 2nd Brigade Commander, described how his units approaching from the north fell upon hundreds of Medina Division armored vehicles, artillery pieces, and other combat equipment, that were mostly oriented toward the south. The Iraqis were obviously caught by surprise,

---

[17] See John Gordon IV and Bruce R. Pirnie, "'Everybody Wanted Tanks': Heavy Forces in Operation *Iraqi Freedom*," *Joint Forces Quarterly*, Issue 39, 4th Quarter 2005, pp. 84–90.

[18] MacKinnon (2003).

[19] Interview with Lieutenant General McKiernan (2004).

[20] Interview with Lieutenant General Wallace (2004).

and the enemy tanks and BMPs (*Bronevaya Maschina Piekhota*) that attempted to turn around and fight were quickly destroyed:

> I think the fact we were able to come in behind him really provided a huge advantage to us. . . . [The Iraqis] are not very agile. They can't adjust their formation and react to developing situations on the battlefield. . . . I think we just overwhelmed them with the speed and firepower we brought, as [the enemy commander] basically became paralyzed and was not able to command and control and move his forces.[21]

While Colonel Perkins could not tell how many of the Iraqi vehicles were still occupied at the time of the attack, he did observe piles of clothing and boots along the road. He believed the 2nd Brigade's assault produced a "psychological impact" whereby the destruction of a tank at the rear of the Iraqi position, resulted in "the guy half-mile down the road saying, 'OK, that's it, I'm out'":

> I think the desertion was occurring as we're fighting, because we would see literally piles of clothing, like a platoon's worth of clothing, just piled, and guys [are] gone. . . . We'd see a lot of middle-aged males walking away from the battlefield. Some of them would have army boots on, but then they would have civilian undergarment[s].[22]

Colonel Perkins, whose units also made the April 5th and 7th "Thunder Runs" into Baghdad, observed that most of the fighting that occurred with the Medina Division and in Baghdad involved engagements with individual armored vehicles and small enemy-troop elements, rather than with cohesive and coordinated larger units:

> Even when we went into Baghdad, [we engaged in] very tenacious fighting [with individuals]. But [the problem was] they just

---

[21] Interview with Colonel David Perkins, "The Invasion of Iraq: An Oral History," *Frontline*, PBS, posted March 9, 2004. Online at http://www.pbs.org/wgbh/pages/frontline/shows/invasion/interviews/perkins.html (as of February 27, 2004).

[22] Interview with Colonel David Perkins (2004).

couldn't bring it together. Warfare is just very complicated stuff. When our brigade just came upon them in three different areas, we were spread out over 50 miles. We just came upon them [with] close air support and artillery. I'm sure it was just more than they could even imagine. It just develops so quickly, and our tanks, our Bradleys are just going through their formation so quickly, that it just becomes obvious that it's hopeless for them. So I'm sure their leadership just basically gave up at that point.[23]

General Omar Abdul Karim, an Iraqi Regular Army commander, confirmed the effects of the fast U.S. armor assault on the forces attempting to defend Baghdad:

We weren't prepared, but it didn't matter because the tank assault was so fast and sudden. . . . The Americans were able to divide and isolate our forces. Nobody had any idea what was going on until it was too late.[24]

---

[23] Interview with Colonel David Perkins (2004).

[24] See Zucchino (2003), p. 1.

CHAPTER SEVEN

Concluding Observations

Four issues relating to OIF deserve further discussion: (1) How the speed and costs of Saddam's overthrow closely tracked prewar predictions, (2) how the extreme weakness of the Iraqi resistance undermines the validity of lessons about military strategy and force sizing that can be drawn from OIF, (3) how Iraqi behavior in OIF paved the way for the insurgency that followed, and (4) how OIF may influence the behavior of future adversaries.

The Coalition's Success Was Achieved Rapidly and at a Low Cost

In terms of the immediate Coalition objective of bringing down Saddam Hussein's regime, OIF was a manifest success. Victory was achieved (1) rapidly and (2) at a comparatively small cost in friendly casualties, both important measures of battlefield accomplishment.

The ease with which the takedown was accomplished was not a surprise to senior U.S. military leaders, as it occurred within the time lines they had forecast. When asked by Secretary of Defense Donald Rumsfeld for their estimates of how long it would take to achieve regime change, General Richard B. Myers, [Myers is a four star] the Chairman of the Joint Chiefs of Staff (JCS), reportedly replied that he thought U.S. forces would get to Baghdad in about two to three weeks, and would take about "30 days in all." General Peter Pace, Vice Chairman of the JCS, estimated that it would take less than a month, assuming that U.S. intelligence about likely large-scale Iraqi capitulations was accurate. CENTCOM Commander General Tommy Franks said the time required to take down the regime would be measured in "weeks[,] not months."[1] These estimates are all close to the 20 days that it actually took to bring about the capture of Baghdad and the collapse of Saddam's regime.[2]

The number of U.S. casualties suffered in OIF also was in general accord with at least the CENTCOM Commander's expectations. General Franks is reported to have told some members of his staff that "he thought there would be fewer tha[n] 1,000 casualties on the U.S. side and probably only several hundred."[3] This tracks closely with the total 681 combat casualties U.S. forces actually suffered prior to May 1, 2003, when President Bush declared the end of significant combat.[4]

But Decisionmakers Should Be Careful About the Lessons They Draw from OIF

Military and civilian decisionmakers should be careful not to draw unwarranted lessons from OIF, particularly the notion that high-tech weaponry and communications will inevitably enable smaller-sized U.S. forces to be decisive against larger-sized but less high-tech enemy forces in future conflicts.[5] Decisionmakers should also be cautious

---

[1] The most optimistic of those responding was Paul Wolfowitz, the Undersecretary of Defense, who estimated that Saddam's regime would be brought down within seven days. See Woodward (2004), pp. 325–326.

[2] Saddam departed Baghdad on April 10, 21 days after the start of OIF, but he and other regime leaders had ceased to command and control Iraqi forces one day earlier.

[3] Woodward (2004), p. 327.

[4] The 681 total casualties included 109 KIA, 30 nonhostile deaths, and 542 wounded in action (WIA). See U.S. Department of Defense, Washington Headquarters, DoD Personnel and Military Casualty Statistics (2006).

[5] When asked how valid it would be to draw lessons from OIF, Lieutenant General James T. Conway responded,

> I think we'd better be careful drawing lessons from the whole of the effort, if you will. I'd have cautioned our headquarters and our decision-makers that this is probably an anomaly, both for the Marine Corps and perhaps for the nation. . . . I also think that

about extrapolating strategic lessons from OIF, such as the proposition that invasions can be conducted at minimal cost in U.S. casualties in the absence of extended preparatory air attacks. The extraordinary battlefield advantages that Coalition forces enjoyed in Iraq during March and April 2003 may not be replicated in future conflicts.

As the following sections show, Coalition forces faced a debilitated Iraqi military establishment in OIF that performed even worse than it had in the Persian Gulf War and that was greatly handicapped by Saddam Hussein's strategic misjudgments, focus on internal threats, poor appointments, and inept battlefield management.

Generally Weak in War, Iraq's Military Performance in OIF Proved Even Worse Than Its Poor Showing in Desert Storm

The Iraqi military has proved to be an extremely weak and inept foe in conventional conflicts with U.S. forces. Moreover, even when fighting internal or other external enemies, the Iraqi military's performance has often proved less than competent.[6] Among other shortcomings, Iraqi forces in all past conflicts have consistently manifested an extremely poor capability at the tactical level and a marked inability to fight battles of maneuver.

The Iraqi performance in the 1948 War of Israeli Independence was very poor. In both the 1967 Six Day War and the 1973 October War, the Iraqi performance was judged to be "worse" than that of any of the other Arab armies participating in those conflicts.[7] The Iraqi military in the 1980–1988 Iran-Iraq War initially performed extremely ineptly. However, Iraqi performance improved in the later stages of

---

we should not formulate changes to the force structure based on what has now been a couple of fights against Iraqis. I don't think [they had a] terribly efficient army. I think both the Gulf War and this Operation Iraqi Freedom will show us that (Interview with Lieutenant General Conway, 2004).

[6] Even when fighting their Kurdish countrymen, Iraqi forces have displayed tactical incompetence. See Pollack (2002a), p. 155.

[7] Pollack (2002a), pp. 155 and 173.

the conflict, albeit against an inferiorly armed and badly outnumbered Iranian foe.[8]

Many of the Iraqi military shortcomings evident in OIF paralleled those observed 12 years earlier in Desert Storm. Poor morale was also endemic in the earlier conflict, particularly within the Iraqi Regular Army. The causes of the low morale in that conflict included the Iraqi troops' war weariness, concerns about Iraq's military inferiority, belief that the occupation of Kuwait was not a just or sufficient cause for war, and conviction that defeat was inevitable. The 38-day Coalition air campaign that preceded the ground campaign in 1991 also severely eroded the Iraqi will to resist. Indeed, some 40 percent of the estimated 400,000 Iraqi troops deployed in the KTO deserted home even before the start of the ground fighting.[9]

During the 100-hour ground campaign, most Iraqi units either surrendered after little or nor resistance or fled the battlefield. More than 85,000 Iraqi officers and enlisted personnel were captured by or surrendered to Coalition forces. However, a few Republican Guard and Regular Army elements did fight, particularly as they attempted to screen the withdrawal of other Iraqi units from the KTO.[10]

The Iraqi military establishment that the Coalition faced in OIF was substantially more debilitated and hollow than was the enemy the United States and its allies faced in 1991. So too, the U.S capability to inflict lethal precision strikes on enemy forces was substantially greater in OIF than in Desert Storm. As a consequence, the imbalances in the correlation of forces that had so greatly disadvantaged the Iraqi side in the 1991 Persian Gulf War became even more pronounced in OIF. An

---

[8]   By early 1988, Iraq had about 1,000,000 men under arms, whereas Iran could field only some 600,000. At the points of attack, the Iraqi manpower advantages were often enormous, with the Iraqi side enjoying favorable "force ratios of ten to one, twenty to one, and even fifty to one in certain categories not uncommon." The Iraqi advantage in combat equipment was also huge; Iraq possessed some 4,000 functional tanks while Iran could muster fewer than 1,000. The disparity in combat aircraft was even greater, as Iraq had over 600 and Iran "could surge less than 50" (Pollack, 2002a, pp. 231–232).

[9]   Hosmer (2002), pp. 77–137.

[10]   Hosmer (2002), pp. 152–177.

Iraqi battlefield performance that was poor in 1991 was even worse in 2003. Even though the Iraqis were countering an invasion of their homeland in OIF and the ground fighting lasted much longer than in the Persian Gulf War, the intensity of the resistance in OIF (as measured by the number of troops killed per days of combat) was weaker than the 1991 conflict. During the four days of ground combat in the Persian Gulf War, U.S. Army and Marine forces lost a total 63 killed as compared with the 103 Army and Marine soldiers killed in combat during the nearly 40 days of fighting during March and April 2003.[11] Similarly, as against the possible 10,000 or so Iraqi military estimated to have been killed during ground combat in Desert Storm, between 4,350 and 6,050 Iraqi military personnel are estimated to have died during the U.S. invasion in spring 2003.[12]

The number of enemy units that even attempted to resist was low in both conflicts. In Desert Storm, imagery analysis of the immediate postconflict battlefield, showed that only about 15 percent of Iraqi tanks and APCs attempted to redeploy to fight or even face the Coalition ground attack.[13] In OIF, Lieutenant General Hamdani, the Republican Guard II Corps Commander, estimated that only about 15 percent of Iraqi forces actually fought.[14] However, this estimate seems high, even for the Iraqi forces in II Corps. It is certainly far too high for Iraqi Regular Army and Republican Guard forces as a whole, based on the limited fighting seen on the battlefield and the information about nonresistance provided by interviews with Iraqi officers and enlisted personnel.

---

[11] For Army and Marine losses in Desert Storm, see Hosmer (2002), p. 175. Saddam's regime collapsed on April 9; however, U.S. forces continued to be killed in mopping-up operations, suffering eight KIAs between April 10 and April 25. U.S. Department of Defense, Washington Headquarters, DoD Personnel and Military Casualty Statistics, 2006.

[12] Probably about 5,000 of these Iraqi KIAs were killed during the 38-day bombing campaign that preceded the Desert Storm ground offensive. See Hosmer (2002), p. 171, and "Casualties," *The Washington Post*, April 23, 2005, p. A14.

[13] See Hosmer (2002), pp. 59 and 163–165.

[14] Interview with Lieutenant General Hamdani (2004).

The rapid collapse of the Republican Guard forces was a major surprise to U.S. commanders and to many senior Iraqi officers.[15] Most Republican Guard units had disintegrated as cohesive fighting units even before they were engaged by U.S. ground forces. Commenting on the absence of significant organized opposition from the Republican Guard, Colonel William F. Grimsley, who commanded the 1st Brigade, 3rd Infantry Division, stated, "We never really found any cohesive unit of any brigade of any Republican Guard division." Instead, his troops encountered a mixture of "Baath Party fanatics, paramilitary fighters and members of different Republican Guard divisions, including the Nebuchadnezzar, the Adnan and the Medina."[16]

General Wallace described the surprisingly weak opposition and large number of abandoned and damaged vehicles his forces encountered as they approached Baghdad:

[As we got] closer to Baghdad, we expected a tougher fight. We expected the Republican Guard to be the formation that we were going to have to deal with, and we expected it to be a much more difficult and much more resolute defense. What it turned out to be was a few organizations that fought very small engagements, albeit somewhat violent. But in terms of a coherent defense, in terms of an entire enemy division . . . which was coming from the west, it just didn't appear to us.

And what we found when we got up there was a large number of abandoned vehicles, a large number of vehicles that had apparently been struck by either Coalition [forces], or Coalition air power, or army aviation, or our own direct fire systems, or our own indirect fire systems that appeared to have been abandoned when they were struck. It seemed to me that the will of the enemy to fight seemed to decay rather rapidly, which is something we didn't anticipate nor should we have anticipated. . . .[17]

---

[15] See Interview with Lieutenant General Wallace (2004).

[16] Branigin (2003), p. A25.

[17] Interview with Lieutenant General Wallace (2004).

The Coalition Was Fortunate That Saddam Acted As He Did

The Coalition benefited greatly both from what Saddam Hussein did and from what he did not do in the run-up to and conduct of OIF. The Iraqi leader's strategic misjudgments, propensity to focus on internal threats, poor defensive schemes and command appointments, and inept battlefield management significantly weakened the Iraqi military's capability to mount even a semblance of an effective defense. Indeed, it is hard to think of other actions that Saddam might have taken, short of unconditional surrender, that would have proven more beneficial to the Coalition cause than the policies and practices that he actually adopted.

But what Saddam did not do was perhaps even more important. Had the Iraqi leader held a less benign view of the Coalition's intentions and recognized early on that his regime was in serious peril, he might have adopted scorched-earth tactics and other courses of action that could have increased the costs of OIF to both the Coalition and to the Iraqi people.

Had he understood that the fighting will and combat capability of his Republican Guard and Regular Army forces were at best problematic, he might have discarded any thoughts of successful Iraqi counterattacks and ordered preemptive actions to slow any Coalition advance, including the systematic mining of roads, destruction of bridges, and breaching of dams to inundate likely routes of advance. Similarly, had Saddam recognized that Baghdad could not be defended effectively by forces positioned outside the capital, he might have prepared robust defensive positions inside the capital and taken the risk of positioning Republican Guard armored and infantry divisions inside the city to conduct a last-ditch urban defense. Finally, if he believed it might help preserve his regime, Saddam might have ordered the torching of all the oil wells and the destruction of the various other oil-production facilities in both the southern Rumaila and northern Kirkuk oil fields.

Coalition leaders had anticipated the actions discussed above and had prepared their forces to clear minefields, erect their own bridges, and deal with a "fortress Baghdad."[18] Actions were taken to attempt

---

[18] See Interview with Lieutenant General McKiernan (2004).

to seize both the southern Rumaila oil facilities before they could be destroyed and the Hadithah Dam north of Karbala before it could be breached. However, had Saddam acted early enough and prepared their demolition prior to the outbreak of hostilities, the destruction of the oil facilities and the breaching of the dam probably could not have been prevented.

Had Saddam taken such actions, the fighting in OIF would have been more protracted and Coalition casualties would no doubt have been higher. The systematic dropping of bridges, inundating of the countryside, and torching of oil fields also would have significantly increased the costs of post-war reconstruction in Iraq. The latter two actions, of course, also would have caused significant damage to Iraq's environment.

However, none of these actions would have prevented a Coalition victory or saved Saddam's regime. Nor would an improved Iraqi battlefield performance or a less-well-executed Coalition campaign basically have changed the outcome. From the vantage point of hindsight, the Coalition superiority in OIF was such that there was a substantial margin for error in the takedown phase of the operation.

Some Iraqi senior officers believed they could and should have prolonged the fight.[19] But they readily acknowledged the ultimate futility of attempts at resistance. As the former Iraqi defense minister saw it,

> [e]ven if Iraq's military performed better during Operation Iraqi [F]reedom, Iraq would only have increased the number of Coalition casualties without altering the war's outcome. . . .[20]

---

[19] As Lieutenant General Hamdani put it, "We might have fought for [a] longer time and could have delayed the enemy and forced him to pay [a] heavy price, so as to have justice for the Iraqi people and armed forces from [a] historic point of view" (Interview with Lieutenant General Hamdani, 2004).

[20] Duelfer (2004), p. 32.

OIF Set the Stage for the Insurgency That Followed

Despite speculation to the contrary, Saddam did not plan for a protracted guerrilla war after an Iraqi defeat in the conventional conflict.[21] As previously noted, Saddam did not believe his regime would
be overthrown or that Coalition forces would seize Baghdad. Instead,
he believed his forces would be able to hold out long enough to build
political pressures sufficient to cause the Coalition to accept a political
solution that would leave him in power.[22] Saddam was probably as surprised as any Iraqi when U.S. forces entered Baghdad.[23] He attributed
the collapse of the Iraqi defenses to "betrayal," a charge that was also
echoed by his daughter Raghad.[24]

According to the account of Uday Hussein's personal bodyguard,
Saddam, following the entry of U.S. forces into the capital, told members of a crowd outside a mosque in the Adhamiya area of Baghdad:

> What can I do? I trusted the commanders but they were traitors
> and they betrayed Iraq. But we hope that, before long, we will be
> back in power and everything will be fixed.[25]

---

[21] Investigators considered the possibility that Saddam all along intended to make a strategic withdrawal and fight a guerrilla war, but they said they could find no evidence of such
a strategy from interrogations or documents. See Moore (2003), p. A1, and Coll (2003),
p. A1.

[22] Duelfer (2004), p. 68.

[23] The Iraqi leader was surprised by the swiftness of the Iraqi defeat (see Duelfer, 2004,
p. 68).

[24] See Frontline Transcript (2004), p. 35. Saddam's daughter Raghad asserted in a postwar
interview in Jordan that the rapid fall of Baghdad was due to "treason" in high places. As she
described it: "Regrettably, the people in whom he [Saddam] placed his full trust and whom
he considered his right-hand men were the main sources of treason" ("Al-Arabiyah TV Interviews Saddam's Daughter Raghad," 2003).

[25] See Philp (2003).

Iraqi Actions to Fend Off the Invasion Helped Shape and Promote the Insurgency That Followed

Although not prompted by considerations of a postwar resistance, a number of Iraqi actions before and during OIF helped to facilitate and shape the insurgency that has emerged in Iraq, including

- **The large-scale arming of Ba'athist and tribal loyalists before OIF.** Saddam expected these loyalists to employ guerrilla tactics to oppose any invading forces' attempts to occupy Iraq's cities and towns. The provision of additional weapons to these groups increased the pool of armed regime loyalists who could later fight against a new Iraqi government and Coalition occupation forces.
- **The widespread dispersal of munitions and weapon stockpiles to reduce their vulnerability to destruction by Coalition bombing.** These prewar dispersals, combined with those that had taken place previously, ensured that weapons and explosives would be easily available throughout the country.
- **The release of large numbers of criminals from Iraqi prisons shortly before the war.** These criminal elements have contributed to the general lawlessness that now pervades Iraq and, in some cases, have also actively participated in the insurgency.
- **The movement into Iraq of thousands of foreign jihadists from a number of Middle Eastern and other countries to join the armed struggle against the Coalition invasion.** Some of these foreign jihadists survived the war and probably remained in Iraq to fight the occupation.[26] Building on this earlier precedent, jihadists continue to be recruited in foreign lands and infiltrated into Iraq across its porous borders.
- **The stationing in urban areas of Fedayeen Saddam and Ba'athist Militias that were prepared to deal harshly with anti-regime collaborators and fight tenaciously against the foreign invaders.** The demonstrated willingness of Fedayeen Saddam fighters

---

[26] Some jihadists were unable to return to their home countries because they lacked the money for the trip or because they were without their passports, which had been taken from when they entered Iraq. See Stalinsky (2003).

to mount near-suicidal attacks against U.S. armored elements should have alerted senior U.S. decisionmakers to the possibility that a similarly fanatical resistance might also confront U.S. occupation forces. Some of the Fedayeen Saddam fighters and Ba'athist militiamen who survived the war were among the first to take up arms against the occupation.[27]

- **The employment of unconventional tactics and weapons that eventually would become the hallmarks of Iraqi insurgent operations.** Guerrilla-style ambushes along transit routes, the use of roadside bombs, and suicide attacks with vehicle-borne improvised explosive devices are a few examples.[28]

The Nature of the Iraqi Collapse Impaired Stability Operations

Importantly, the rise of the insurgency in Iraq was also facilitated by the magnitude and nature of the Iraqi collapse, which was marked by the desertion of virtually the entire Iraqi military, security, and governmental structure. By the time Saddam fled Baghdad on April 10, hundreds of thousands of Iraqi military and civilian-government personnel, including all the country's senior military leaders and Saddam's key associates, had abandoned their posts and either returned to their homes or gone into hiding.

This massive flight from duty stations had two major consequences:

- First, it released into the Iraqi countryside numerous former military officers and rank-and-file militia fighters, security and intelligence personnel, and Ba'athist officials who possessed the skills, resources, and potential motivation to mount and sustain a

---

[27] According to some Iraqi former military sources, the Ba'ath Party and Fedayeen Saddam militiamen and the foreign jihadists who had regrouped after the fall of Baghdad, were behind most of the attacks against U.S. forces in 2003. See Moore (2003), p. A1. Also, see Ahmed S. Hashim, *Insurgency and Counter-Insurgency in Iraq*, Ithaca, N.Y.: Cornell University Press, 2006, pp. 48, 117, 152, and 155.

[28] The 3rd Infantry Division and the Marines suffered a number of casualties from car bomber attacks. The Marines also had tanks knocked out by this means of attack. See Interview with Lieutenant General Conway (2004). Also, see Gordon and Trainor (2006a), pp. 348, 372, 384, and 500.

resistance against the occupation. The Coalition was able to identify, vet, and incarcerate only a small fraction of these potential
oppositionists.[29]
- Second, it deprived the Coalition of the indigenous military forces
  and civilian officials that the Coalition planners had counted on
  to help stabilize and secure Iraq. Realizing that their own forces
  might be overstretched, U.S. commanders planned to use surrendered units of the Iraqi Regular Army and police to help maintain
  order, control the borders, and perform the other security tasks
  that Coalition forces might face after the war.[30]

The small size of the OIF invasion force magnified the harmful
effects of the absence of any compensating indigenous assets. Indeed,
the rapid growth of the insurgency in Iraq may be traced in part to the
decision by senior U.S. leaders to invade and occupy the country with
only a minimally sized force.[31]

Central to the "decision to limit the amount of combat power
deployed into the theater" was the fundamental assumption that "the
Iraqi military would not resist."[32] There was a corollary assumption

---

[29] Among those at large were former members of the Al Ghafiqi Project (M21 Directorate)
of the Iraqi Intelligence Service, commonly known as the Mukhabarat. The Al Ghafiqi Project existed to make improvised explosive devices (IEDs) and other explosive devices for the
IIS to use in assassination and demolition operations. See Duelfer (2004), p. 81.

[30] Assumed in Lieutenant General McKiernan's plan for the postwar effort that would
follow the collapse of Saddam's regime was that "U.S. forces would rely on the Iraqi military, the Iraqi police and existing legal system, provincial governments, and Iraqi ministries
to maintain order and administer the country" (Gordon and Trainor, 2006a, pp. 105 and
145).

[31] Including the 20,000 men of the British 1st Armored Division, the initial Coalition invasion force totaled about 145,000 troops. This was less than half the size of the some 300,000-
man invasion force specified in an earlier Iraq invasion plan (Desert Crossing), which had
been produced during General Anthony Zinni's 1997–2000 tenure as CENTCOM Commander. See Thomas E. Ricks, Fiasco: The American Military Adventure in Iraq, New York:
The Penguin Press, 2006, p. 117, and "Gen. Zinni: 'They've Screwed Up,'" 60 Minutes, CBS
News, May 21, 2004 (online at http://www.cbsnews.com/stories/2004/05/21/60minutes/
printable618896.shtml [as of September 28, 2006]).

[32] See Fontenot, Degen, and Tohn (2004), p. 69.

that a relatively small force would also be capable of handling any post-war contingencies that might arise.

Despite the pre-invasion testimony of General Eric Shinseki, the Army Chief of Staff, that a significant ground force presence "on the order of several hundred thousand soldiers" probably would be needed to establish "post-hostilities control" over Iraq, senior U.S. defense officials assumed that a force sufficient to take down Saddam's regime would be sufficient to police the country.[33]

Paul Wolfowitz, the Deputy Secretary of Defense, voiced this view in his testimony before Congress on March 27, 2003. Directly rebutting General Shinseki's estimate, Wolfowitz stated:

> But some of the higher-end predictions that we have been hearing recently, such as the notion that it will take several hundred thousand U.S. troops to provide stability in post-Saddam Iraq, are wildly off the mark. First, it's hard to conceive that it would take more forces to provide stability in post-Saddam Iraq than it would take to conduct the war itself and to secure the surrender of Saddam's security forces and his army. Hard to imagine.[34]

But Saddam's forces did not behave in the manner Secretary Wolfowitz and others had expected. Indeed, a number of the developments that accompanied the demise of Saddam's regime clearly were not anticipated by U.S. military and civilian leaders. The U.S. leaders had expected large-scale Iraqi unit surrenders, a welcoming Iraqi public, and at least some elements of the Iraqi government to remain in place.[35] Instead, the vast majority of Iraqi military and security forces chose to desert rather than surrender; much of the Iraqi public, while

---

[33] See testimony of General Shinseki before the Senate Armed Services Committee in late February 2003, quoted in Frontline Transcript (2004), p. 18.

[34] See Frontline Transcript (2004), p. 18.

[35] For expectations about large numbers of enemy prisoners of war in Iraq, see Fontenot, Degen, and Tohn (2004), p. 69. For Central Intelligence Agency (CIA) expectations that the Iraqi public would warmly greet U.S. troops, see "CIA Expected Iraqis to Wave U.S. Flags After Invasion," World News from AP [Associated Press], October 20, 2004. Online at http://sg.news.yahoo.com/041020/1/3nvx3.html (as of November 2004).

pleased to see Saddam's departure, proved reluctant to embrace a foreign occupation; and the governmental structure throughout the non-Kurdish areas of Iraq totally dissolved. Without the active assistance of organized Iraqi military and police forces, coalition troops lacked the numerical strength to promptly stabilize the country.[36]

Commenting on his surprise at the absence of an Iraqi infrastructure, General Wallace observed:

> I give no credit to the politicians for detailed Phase Four (the reconstruction of Iraq) planning. But I don't think that we, the military, did a very good job of anticipating [that] either. I don't think that any of us either could have [anticipated] or did anticipate the total collapse of this regime and the psychological impact it had on the entire nation. When we arrived in Baghdad, everybody had gone home. The regime officials were gone; the folks that provided security of the ministry buildings had gone; the folks that operated the water treatment plants and the electricity grid and the water purification plants were gone.
>
> I for one did not anticipate our presence being such a traumatic influence on the entire population. We expected there to be some degree of infrastructure left in the city, in terms of intellectual infrastructure, in terms of running the city infrastructure, in terms of running the government infrastructure. But what in fact happened, which was unanticipated at least in [my mind], is that when [we] decapitated the regime, everything below it fell apart. I'm not sure that we could have anticipated that. . . .[37]

Looting Was a Surprising Result. Similarly, U.S. leaders were obviously also surprised by the massive looting that broke out in Baghdad and other locales once Saddam's security apparatus in the area had dissolved. That this was unexpected is in itself surprising in that the last U.S. military takedown of a regime, the 1989 ouster of Noriega in

---

[36] See Gordon and Trainor (2006a), pp. 460–462 and 465–470.

[37] Interview with Lieutenant General Wallace (2004).

Panama, also was followed by massive looting that was hugely costly to the Panamanian economy.[38]

The looting, which began on a small scale, quickly escalated and got out of hand. U.S. forces were slow to attempt to stop it, partly because they initially had no orders to do so and partly because the United States and its Coalition partners lacked sufficient forces to do so.[39] Attempting to stop the looting might also have required the shooting of a large number of civilians, which would have been unacceptable politically. The task of imposing control was also impaired by the dearth of military police in the occupation force.[40] Clearly, the absence

---

[38] The Panama looting was a surprise to General Max Thurman, the Southern Command (SOUTHCOM) Commander, who said he would have brought more military police forces into Panama during Operation Just Cause had he anticipated it. According to one account, the losses from the looting in Panama ranged from "$1 billion to $2 billion." See Richard H. Shultz, Jr., "The Post-Conflict Use of Military Forces: Lessons from Panama, 1989–91," *The Journal of Strategic Studies*, June 1993, p. 154.

[39] According to Todd Purdum of *The New York Times*, "When Iraqis would ask U.S. forces why they weren't trying to stop the looting, the answer was clear. They just didn't have enough people; they couldn't do it." When Thomas Ricks of *The Washington Post*, asked members of the 3rd Infantry Division in Baghdad why they hadn't moved against the looters, he was told that they had "basically stayed in their fighting positions" because "they had no orders to do anything else," and because they felt "under-resourced." "They were tired, they just fought a war. They didn't have a lot of people. Even if you want to establish a presence, a city of 5 million will soak up 20,000 soldiers. So they really were not prepared to do the larger mission of presence, that ultimately was needed." See Interview with Ricks (2004) and Interview with Todd Purdum, "The Invasion of Iraq: An Oral History," *Frontline*, PBS, posted March 9, 2004. Online at http://www.pbs.org/wgbh/pages/frontline/shows/invasion/interviews/ricks.html and http://www.pbs.org/wgbh/pages/frontline/shows/invasion/interviews/purdum.html (as of February 27, 2004). Lieutenant General Jay Garner, U.S. Army (Ret.), who arrived in Baghdad on April 21, 2003, to head the first occupation government in Iraq, stated in a November 2003 interview with the British Broadcasting Corporation (BBC) that "If we did it over again, we probably would have put more dismounted infantrymen in Baghdad and maybe more troops there" ("Jay Garner's November 25th Interview with the BBC," Associated Press, last modified on November 26, 2003. Online at http://www.narsil.org/war_on_iraq/garner_bbc.html [as of December 1, 2003]).

[40] Prewar planning did not envision using military police (MP) to guard Iraqi government facilities or control the Iraqi population. Their "specified and implied tasks" were to include "EPW operations, high-value asset (HVA) security, area security operations, and main supply route (MSR) regulation and enforcement." However, the available manning for even some of these tasks was reduced when "it became obvious that there would be significantly

138 Why the Iraqi Resistance to the Coalition Invasion Was So Weak

of an "overwhelming" U.S. military presence in country when Saddam's regime collapsed allowed widespread lawlessness to take root.[41]

The major effects of the looting appear to have been fourfold: (1) Looting made the reconstruction of Iraq significantly more difficult and costly, (2) it resulted in a radical decline in the quality of life for the Iraqis, (3) it shook the Iraqi public's confidence in the American occupation, and (4) it gave encouragement and momentum to elements who would actively oppose the Coalition occupation.[42]

The absence of effective security in the days immediately after Saddam's regime collapsed caused palpable damage to the image of the American occupation forces that "would endure and worsen in the weeks to come." As one Baghdad citizen expressed his outrage, "This is what America has brought us—looting and destruction."[43]

The absence of an adequate ground-force presence also prevented the Coalition from monitoring Iraq's porous borders and guarding Iraqi munitions stocks. As a consequence, many of the numerous unguarded and widely dispersed Iraqi military munitions and weapon stockpiles were looted during the period, which provided would-be insurgents and terrorists the opportunity to establish hundreds of hidden caches of RPGs, automatic and crew-served weapons, and bomb-making materials.

The lessons for future U.S. war planners seem clear: When taking down an enemy government or otherwise invading a foreign land, U.S. forces must be both appropriately configured and sufficiently robust to promptly establish firm control over the areas they occupy, guard

---

fewer MP units in-theater when the war started than originally planned based on the new force packaging decisions" (Fontenot, Degen, and Tohn, 2004, p. 70).

[41] See statement of Thomas White, Secretary of the Army, 2001–2003, in Frontline Transcript (2004), p. 38.

[42] See Interview with Thomas Ricks (2004). For views on the effects of looting and lawlessness, see Interview with former Secretary White in Frontline Transcript (2004) and Interview with Todd Purdum (2004). Also see Gordon and Trainor (2006a), pp. 467–469.

[43] Quoted in Todd S. Purdum, *A Time of Our Choosing*, New York: Henry Holt and Company, 2003, p. 217.

national borders, and secure enemy arms depots and other sensitive sites.

Some Resistance Was Probably Inevitable. Clearly, factors other than the paucity of Coalition occupation troops also facilitated the growth of the insurgency. Prominent among these were the May 2003 decisions by the Coalition Provisional Authority (CPA) to disband all Iraqi military organizations—an action justified, in part, on the grounds that looters had demolished Iraq's military bases[44]—and its decision to ban all full members of the Ba'ath Party from any public employment, including service in the new Iraqi army. Both actions created pools of humiliated,[45] unemployed, and otherwise disgruntled men who would constitute potential sources of recruits for the insurgency.[46]

---

[44] CPA officials argued that, if they had attempted to call back members of the former Iraqi armed forces, there would have been no place to house them. As Walter Slocombe of the CPA described it:

> When the Iraqi army took off for home, its soldiers took any gear of possible worth along with them—not just military equipment but trucks, furniture and everything of any use. What the fleeing soldiers did not take, the civilian population looted from abandoned bases and camps. Looters and scavengers literally took not just the kitchen sinks but the pipes from the walls and the tiles that covered the kitchen floors. Rehabilitating these facilities for use by Coalition forces or by new Iraqi security organizations has taken months of hard work and millions of dollars. Had a recall somehow evoked a response, we would have found ourselves not with 500,000 disciplined soldiers ready to impose order under U.S. command but with 500,000 refugees needing shelter, food, uniforms, weapons and a good many other things—just to survive. Instead of being a help to the American and other forces, they would have been a huge burden (Slocombe, 2003, p. A29).

[45] For a discussion of "humiliation" as a catalyst for insurgency in Iraq, see Victoria Fontan, "Polarization Between Occupier and Occupied in Post-Saddam Iraq: Colonial Humiliation and the Formation of Political Violence," *Terrorism and Political Violence*, Vol. 18, 2006, pp. 217–238.

[46] Retired Lieutenant General Jay Garner, former Director of the Office of Reconstruction and Humanitarian Assistance (ORHA), who was originally responsible for the postwar administration in Iraq, believed the decision to disband the Iraqi army "was a mistake" because it threw hundreds of thousands of Iraqi breadwinners out of work and provided a body of potential recruits for the insurgency. General Garner also felt that the de-Ba'athification order went too far, encompassing too many former Ba'athists. He warned Ambassador Paul L. Bremer, the newly appointed head of the CPA, that the action would drive some 30,000 to 50,000 Ba'athists underground. Although the actual effect may have been less severe than General Garner feared, the de-Ba'athification order undoubtedly was

All this said, even if the United States had sent larger forces to Iraq and had not disbanded the Iraqi military, and indeed even if it had taken other actions to dissuade potential opposition, such as holding early elections, some degree of armed resistance in Iraq was probably inevitable. The number of former regime elements at large after the war with the motivation and capability to attack U.S. forces was sufficient in itself to ensure some armed opposition. Numerous other Iraqis were also motivated to oppose the occupation and any Iraqis who aligned themselves with it, including the Sunni Arabs who resented losing the ascendant position they once enjoyed under Saddam's rule and the many Iraqis who considered it their nationalist or religious duty to actively oppose the occupation of their country.

However, a substantially larger U.S. military force at the outset could have restricted the looting, guarded munitions sites and borders, and significantly dampened the lawlessness that swept over Iraq. These and other actions aimed at preempting and reducing opposition, such as more-restrained and culturally sensitive U.S. troop behavior, probably could have prevented the insurgency from gaining as strong a foothold in Iraq as it now enjoys.

How OIF May Influence the Behavior of the United States' Future Adversaries

Commenting on the devastating conventional defeat the United States had inflicted on Iraq in the 1991 Gulf War, an Indian minister of defense once famously observed, "Don't fight the United States unless you have nuclear weapons."[47] The defense minister's meaning, of course, was that a nuclear deterrent was needed if a country was to ward off submitting to coercion or catastrophic defeat by technologi-

---

an additional reason for some former regime elements to take up arms against the Coalition. RAND staff interview with Jay Garner, Chief of ORHA, March 23, 2004, and "Jay Garner's November 25th Interview with the BBC," 2003.

[47] Quoted in Les Aspin, "From Deterrence to Denuking: Dealing with Proliferation in the 1990s," House Armed Services Committee Memorandum, Washington, D.C.: U.S. House of Representatives, Committee on Armed Services, February 18, 1992.

cally advanced U.S. conventional forces. Indeed, this was one of the reasons Saddam Hussein wanted nuclear weapons.[48]

Twelve years later, countries that consider themselves to be potential future military adversaries of the United States are likely to share this view, given the rout of Iraqi forces in 2003. In this sense, OIF may constitute an additional spur to nuclear proliferation in countries such as Iran and North Korea. However, OIF also carried another lesson for potential adversaries: that the United States is willing to take military action, including the takedown of hostile governments, to prevent "rogue" states from acquiring or possessing WMD. The takedown of Saddam's regime was probably one of the factors that contributed to Colonel Muammar Qaddafi's decision on December 19, 2003, to abandon Libya's WMD programs.[49]

Another major, downside lesson that potential adversaries could draw from OIF is that their armor, mechanized, and infantry forces— even if modernized—cannot effectively fight U.S. ground forces, so long as U.S. forces have air supremacy. The dilemma enemy commanders face (and one that some Iraqi commanders well understood)

---

[48] Saddam considered nuclear programs as essential to obtaining political freedom at the international level and to "compete with powerful and antagonistic neighbors; to him nuclear weapons were necessary for Iraq to survive." In a conversation (of an unknown date) with Tariq Aziz and other senior officials, Saddam opined, "The existence of the nuclear weapons in other countries makes the USA and Europe get worried. Having nuclear weapons in these areas, with their economic situation known by the US, gives these countries a chance to face the European countries and the Americans" (Duelfer, 2004, p. 26).

[49] Other factors probably weighed more heavily in Qaddafi's decision, particularly his concern to rid Libya of the international sanctions that had been preventing foreign investment in Libya and inhibiting the modernization and expansion of Libya's petroleum industry. The international community's assurance that it was seeking "policy change" and not "regime change" in Libya also contributed to the success of its coercive diplomacy. Some former U.S. officials hold that the Bush administration simply "completed a diplomatic game plan initiated by Clinton" and that "Libyan disarmament did not require a war in Iraq." However, others point to the "demonstration effects" of the use of force in Iraq and Afghanistan, which helped to "concentrate Qaddafi's mind," clarify Libya's choices, and accelerate Qaddafi's decisionmaking with regard to WMD. See Bruce W. Jentleson and Christopher A. Whytock, "Who 'Won' Libya?" *International Security*, Vol. 30, No. 3, Winter 2005/06, pp. 47–86; Martin Indyk, "FOREIGN POLICY: Was Kadafi Scared Straight? The Record Says No," *Los Angeles Times*, March 28, 2004, p. M.3; and Flynt Leverett, "Why Libya Gave Up on the Bomb," *The New York Times*, January 23, 2004, p. A23.

is that if they disperse their armor, artillery, and other heavy weapons to reduce their vulnerability to U.S. air attack, they will lack the mass to withstand U.S. armored attacks. However, if they concentrate their heavy weapons, they will risk rapid attrition from precision U.S. air attacks.

As a consequence, enemy leaders can be expected to attach high priority to devising ways to deny U.S. forces air supremacy or, at least, to reduce the adverse effects of that supremacy. Among other approaches, they are likely to seek capabilities that will upgrade the effectiveness of their own air defenses and improve their ability to deny U.S. aircraft the use of proximate air bases. To make U.S. invasions of their own territory more costly and time-consuming, they may adopt warfighting strategies that emphasize urban warfare and call for the deployment of both heavy and infantry units in built-up areas to fight U.S. ground forces from prepared positions.

Enemy leaders may also draw one other important lesson from OIF: Possessing a credible capability to wage protracted insurgent warfare against U.S. invasion and occupation forces has obvious political-military utility. To develop such a capability, enemy leaders would organize, train, and equip ground units for guerrilla-style warfare and position hidden weapons and munitions caches throughout their country. Selected members of the public would also be organized, motivated, and trained to support resistance warfare if the need should arise.

Iran, with its massive volunteer militia force, the Basij Resistance Corps, seems particularly well-postured for such a guerrilla-style defense.[50] Indeed, General Yahya Rahim Safavi, the head of Iran's Revolutionary Guards, may have hinted at such a defensive strategy when he warned that any U.S. attack on Iran would entrap U.S. forces

---

[50] The Iranian's claim that the Basij forces in coastal Hormozgan Province alone number some 200,000. See FBIS Open Source Center, AP20050221000012 Tehran, Keyhan (Internet Version-WWW) in Persian, February 17, 2005, p. 14.

in a new quagmire, "even bigger" than the one they already faced in Iraq.[51]

Enemy leaders may calculate that the very prospect of becoming bogged down in a protracted guerrilla conflict might serve to deter U.S. leaders from mounting an invasion. If deterrence failed, then protracted insurgency might be a promising strategy for imposing sufficient costs on the occupiers to force the United States to withdraw or agree to a political settlement acceptable to the enemy's leadership.[52]

Indeed, whenever U.S. ground forces become engaged with hostile elements in future conflicts, they must anticipate the possibility of a guerrilla-type response from enemy forces. In such contingencies, the United States will need forces that are organized, trained, equipped, and culturally sensitized for counterinsurgency warfare, attributes and capabilities that were unfortunately lacking in may of the U.S. units that first confronted the insurgent resistance in Iraq.

---

[51] See Stefan Smith, "Tehran Mocks U.S. Ability to Win Military Action," *The Washington Times*, April 15, 2006, p. A6.

[52] America's adversaries in all major wars from World War II onward, have counted on protracting the fighting and exacting sufficient U.S. casualties to the point where the U.S. public would turn against a continued military involvement and force a political solution advantageous to the adversary.

Bibliography

"Al-Arabiyah TV Interviews Saddam's Daughter Raghad," Dubai Al-Arabiyah Television in Arabic, August 1, 2003. FBIS Document ID: GMP20030801000231. As of August 24, 2003:
https://portal.rccb.osis.gov/servlet/Repository?encoded=xml_products:
GMP20030801000231

"Armed Forces, Iraq," *Jane's Sentinel Security Assessment—The Gulf States*, January 13, 2003. As of January 20, 2004:
http://sentinel.janes.com/subscriber/sentinel/doc_view_print.jsp?K2DocKey=/content1/jane

Aspin, Les, "From Deterrence to Denuking: Dealing with Proliferation in the 1990s," House Armed Services Committee Memorandum, Washington, D.C.: U.S. House of Representatives, Committee on Armed Services, February 18, 1992.

"Ba'ath Party Entrenched in Saddam's Cult of Personality," *The China Post*, April 4, 2003. As of January 20, 2005:
http://www.rickross.com/reference/general/general539.html

Baker, Peter, "U.S. to Negotiate Capitulation Agreements with Iraqi Military," *The Washington Post*, March 18, 2003. As of June 14, 2007:
http://www-tech.mit.edu/V123/N13/iraq-military.13w.html

Baram, Amatzia, "Would Saddam Husayn Abdicate?," Washington, D.C.: The Brookings Institution, Iraq Memo No. 9, February 4, 2003.

Biddle, Stephen, "Prepared Testimony of Dr. Stephen Biddle, Associate Professor of National Security Studies, U.S. Army War College Strategic Studies Institute," before the House Armed Services Committee, October 21, 2003. As of June 26, 2007:
http://www.globalsecurity.org/military/library/congress/2003_hr/03-10-21biddle.htm

Biddle, Stephen, et al., "Iraq and the Future of Warfare," briefing, Strategic Studies Institute, U.S. Army War College, Carlisle, Pa., August 18, 2003.

Blair, David, "Why the Fedayeen Fight for Their Lives," *Telegraph (UK)*, March 25, 2003b.

————, "145 of My 150 Men Fled, Says Guard Officer," *Telegraph (UK)*, filed April 14, 2003a.

Blix, Hans, *Disarming Iraq*, New York: Pantheon Books, 2004.

Branigin, William, "A Brief, Bitter War for Iraq's Military Officers," *The Washington Post*, April 27, 2003.

"Bush Aides Play Down Effort to Avert War at Last Minute," *The New York Times*, November 7, 2003.

"Casualties," *The Washington Post*, April 23, 2005.

CFLCC—See Combined Forces Land Component Commander.

Chandrasekaran, Rajiv, "Iraq Seeks Meeting with U.N. Inspectors," *The Washington Post*, March 16, 2003.

————, "Iraq Arms Civilians as Second Line of Defense Against U.S.," *The Washington Post*, February 5, 2003.

Chapman, Susann, "The 'War' Before the War," *Air Force Magazine*, February 2004.

"CIA Expected Iraqis to Wave U.S. Flags After Invasion," World News from AP, October 20, 2004. As of November 2004:
http://sg.news.yahoo.com/041020/1/3nvx3.html

Coll, Steve, "Hussein Was Sure of Own Survival; Aide Says Confusion Reigned on Eve of War," *The Washington Post*, November 3, 2003.

Combined Forces Land Component Commander (CFLCC) Intelligence Update, briefing, March 23, 2003, 0300Z.

Council on Foreign Relations, "Iraq: What Is the Fedayeen Saddam?" updated March 31, 2003. As of June 14, 2007:
http://www.cfr.org/publication/7698/iraq.html

"Creation of a New Iraqi Army," Coalition Provisional Authority Order Number 22, Baghdad, Iraq, August 18, 2003. As of January 29, 2007:
http://www.cpa-iraq.org/#

Dannreuther, Roland, *The Gulf Conflict: A Political and Strategic Analysis*, London: International Institute for Strategic Studies, Adelphi Paper 264, Winter 1991–1992.

"De-Ba'athification of Iraqi Society," Coalition Provisional Authority Order Number 1, Baghdad, Iraq, May 16, 2003. As of January 29, 2007:
http://www.cpa-iraq.org/#

Dickey, Christopher, "'Mafia State,'" *Newsweek*, January 5, 2006. As of September 6, 2006:
http://www.msnbc.msn.com/id/10728635/site/newsweek/print/1/displaymode/1098/

"Dissolution of Entities," Coalition Provisional Authority Order Number 2, Baghdad, Iraq, May 23, 2003. As of June 26, 2007:
http://www.cpa-iraq.org/regulations/20030921_CPAORD34.pdf

Dodge, Toby, *Inventing Iraq: The Failure of Nation Building and a History Denied*, New York: Columbia University Press, 2003.

Duelfer, Charles, Special Adviser to the Director of Central Intelligence (DCI), *Comprehensive Report of the Special Adviser to the DCI on Iraq's WMD*, Vol. I, September 30, 2004.

"Excerpts from Iraqi Transcripts of Meeting with U.S. Envoy," *The New York Times*, September 23, 1990.

FBIS Open Source Center, AP20050221000012 Tehran, Keyhan (Internet Version-WWW) in Persian, February 17, 2005.

FBIS Trends, FB TM 91-002, January 10, 1991.

Filkins, Dexter, "U.S. Moved to Undermine Iraqi Military Before War," *The New York Times*, August 10, 2003.

Fisk, Robert, "Ruling the Airways—How America Demoralized Iraq's Army," *The Independent (UK)*, May 24, 2003. As of June 10, 2004:
http://web.lexis-nexis.com/universe/document?_m=d94acd59d2a42e30ab941b703 69be73

Fontan, Victoria "Polarization Between Occupier and Occupied in Post-Saddam Iraq: Colonial Humiliation and the Formation of Political Violence," *Terrorism and Political Violence*, Vol. 18, 2006, pp. 217–238.

Fontenot, Colonel Gregory, U.S. Army (Ret.), Lieutenant Colonel E. J. Degen, U.S. Army, and Lieutenant Colonel David Tohn, U.S. Army (Operation Iraqi Freedom Study Group, Office of the Chief of Staff U.S. Army, Washington, D.C.), *On Point*, Fort Leavenworth, Kansas: Combat Studies Institute Press, 2004.

"France Denies Coaxing Saddam on Invasion," Associated Press, November 4, 2003. As of February 27, 2004:
http://www.lasvegassun.com/sunbin/stories/text/2003/nov/04/110405167/html

Franks, Tommy, *American Soldier*, New York: HarperCollins Publishers, Inc., 2004.

Friedman, Herbert A., *Operation Iraqi Freedom*. As of July 10, 2003:
http://www.psywarrior.com/OpnIraqiFreedom.html

Frontline Transcript—See Transcript, "The Invasion of Iraq: An Oral History," *Frontline*, PBS, posted March 9, 2004.

Garner, Jay, Chief of Office of Reconstruction and Humanitarian Assistance (ORHA), RAND staff interview, March 23, 2004.

"Gen. Zinni: 'They've Screwed Up,'" *60 Minutes*, CBS News, May 21, 2004. As of September 28, 2006:
http://www.cbsnews.com/stories/2004/05/21/60minutes/printable618896.shtml

"Good News for Iraqi Soldiers," Coalition Provisional Authority Press Release No. 006, Baghdad, Iraq, June 23, 2003. As of June 14, 2007:
http://www.iraqcoalition.org/pressreleases/23June03PR6_good_news.pdf

Gordon IV, John, and Bruce R. Pirnie, "'Everybody Wanted Tanks': Heavy Forces in Operation Iraqi Freedom," *Joint Forces Quarterly*, Issue 39, 4th Quarter 2005, pp. 84–90.

Gordon, Michael R., and General Bernard E. Trainor, *Cobra II*, New York: Pantheon Books, 2006a.

———, "Iraqi Leader, in Frantic Flight, Eluded U.S. Strikes," *The New York Times*, March 12, 2006b.

Hashim, Ahmed, "Foreign Involvement in the Iraqi Insurgency," *Terrorism Monitor* [The Jamestown Foundation], Vol. 2, Issue 16, August 12, 2004. As of January 29, 2007:
http://www.jamestown.org/print_friendly.php?volume_id=400&issue_id=3047&article_id=2368398

———, *Insurgency and Counter-Insurgency in Iraq*, Ithaca, N.Y.: Cornell University Press, 2006.

Hayes, Stephen F., "Saddam's Terror Camps," *The Weekly Standard*, January 16, 2006. As of January 29, 2007:
http://www.weeklystandard.com/Utilities/printer_preview.asp?idArticle=6550&R=EB3D2AC08

Hosenball, Mark, "Iraq: What in the World Was Saddam Thinking?" *Newsweek*, September 15, 2003.

Hosmer, Stephen T., *Effects of the Coalition Air Campaign Against Iraqi Ground Forces in the Gulf War*, Santa Monica, Calif.: RAND Corporation, 2002 (not available to the general public).

———, *Operations Against Enemy Leaders*, Santa Monica, Calif.: RAND Corporation, MR-1385-AF, 2001. As of January 29, 2007:
http://www.rand.org/pubs/monograph_reports/MR1385/

Indyk, Martin, "FOREIGN POLICY: Was Kadafi Scared Straight? The Record Says No," *Los Angeles Times*, March 28, 2004.

International Institute for Strategic Studies, *The Military Balance*, London: Oxford University Press, 2000–2001.

Interview with Colonel David Perkins, "The Invasion of Iraq: An Oral History," *Frontline*, PBS, posted March 9, 2004. As of February 27, 2004:
http://www.pbs.org/wgbh/pages/frontline/shows/invasion/interviews/perkins.html

Interview with Lieutenant Colonel Ernest "Rock" Marcone, "The Invasion of Iraq: An Oral History," *Frontline*, PBS, posted March 9, 2004. As of February 27, 2004:
http://www.pbs.org/wgbh/pages/frontline/shows/invasion/interviews/marcone. html

Interview with Lieutenant General David D. McKiernan, Commander, 3rd Army and CFLCC, "The Invasion of Iraq: An Oral History," *Frontline*, PBS, posted March 9, 2004. As of February 27, 2004:
http://www.pbs.org/wgbh/pages/frontline/shows/invasion/interviews/mckiernan. html

Interview with Lieutenant General James T. Conway, "The Invasion of Iraq: An Oral History," *Frontline*, PBS, posted March 9, 2004. As of February 27, 2004:
http://www.pbs.org/wgbh/pages/frontline/shows/invasion/interviews/conway.html

Interview with Lieutenant General Raad Al-Hamdani, "The Invasion of Iraq: An Oral History," *Frontline*, PBS, posted March 9, 2004. As of February 27, 2004:
http://www.pbs.org/wgbh/pages/frontline/shows/invasion/interviews/raad.html

Interview with Lieutenant General Wafic Samarrai, "The Gulf War: An Oral History," *Frontline*, PBS, posted January 28, 1997. As of June 26, 2007:
http://www.pbs.org/wgbh/pages/frontline/gulf/oral/samarrai/1.html

Interview with Lieutenant General William Scott Wallace, Commander, V Corps, "The Invasion of Iraq: An Oral History," *Frontline*, PBS, posted March 9, 2004. As of February 27, 2004:
http://www.pbs.org/wgbh/pages/frontline/shows/invasion/interviews/wallace.html

Interview with Thomas E. Ricks, "The Invasion of Iraq: An Oral History," *Frontline*, PBS, posted March 9, 2004. As of February 27, 2004:
http://www.pbs.org/wgbh/pages/frontline/shows/invasion/interviews/ricks.html

Interview with Todd Purdum, "The Invasion of Iraq: An Oral History," *Frontline*, PBS, posted March 9, 2004. As of February 27, 2004:
http://www.pbs.org/wgbh/pages/frontline/shows/invasion/interviews/purdum.html

"Iraqi Militia Defy Conventional Characterization," Associated Press, March 27, 2003. As of June 26, 2007:
http://findarticles.com/p/articles/mi_qn4196/is_20030328/ai_n10866469

Jane's Defence Weekly, February 5, 2003. As of January 29, 2007:
http://www4.janes.com/K2/docprint.jsp?K2DocKey=/content1/janesdata /mags/jdw/history

"Jay Garner's November 25th Interview with the BBC," Associated Press, last modified on November 26, 2003. As of December 1, 2003:
http://www.narsil.org/war_on_iraq/garner_bbc.html

Jehl, Douglas, with Dexter Filkins, "U.S. Moved to Undermine Iraqi Military Before War," *The New York Times*, August 10, 2003.

Jentleson, Bruce W., and Christopher A. Whytock, "Who 'Won' Libya?" *International Security*, Vol. 30, No. 3, Winter 2005/06, pp. 47–86.

Karsh, Efraim, and Inari Rautsi, *Saddam Hussein*, New York: The Free Press, 1991.

Knickmeyer, Ellen, "Rumsfeld Urges Iraqi Leaders Not to Purge Security Forces," *The Washington Post*, April 13, 2005.

Leverett, Flynt, "Why Libya Gave Up on the Bomb," *The New York Times*, January 23, 2004.

MacAskill, Ewen, and Julian Borger, "Iraq 'to Allow Arms Inspectors,'" *The Guardian Weekly* (London), May 2–8, 2002.

MacFarquhar, Neiel, "Hussein, in Rallying His Military, Also Shows Iraqis a Defiant Face," *The New York Times*, March 7, 2005.

MacKinnon, Mark, "Firepower Broke Iraqi Army, Survivor Says," *Toronto Globe and Mail*, April 23, 2003.

Makiya, Kanan, "The Fedayeen Saddam Keep Shia Intifada in Check," *New Perspectives Quarterly*, Vol. 21, Issue 3, Summer 2004.

Martin, Paul, "Iraqi Defense Chief Argued with Saddam," *The Washington Times*, September 21, 2003.

McCarthy, Terry, "What Ever Happened to the Republican Guard?" *Time Magazine*, May 12, 2003.

McGregor, Andrew, "Al-Azhar, Egyptian Islam and the War in Iraq," *Terrorism Monitor* [The Jamestown Foundation], Vol. 2, Issue 12, June 17, 2004. As of June 22, 2004:
http://www.jamestown.org/publications_details

"Meeting with U.S. Envoy: Excerpts from Iraqi Transcripts," *The New York Times*, September 23, 1990.

Moore, Molly, "A Foe That Collapsed from Within," *The Washington Post*, July 20, 2003.

Murray, Williamson, and Robert H. Scales, Jr., *The Iraq War*, Cambridge, Mass.: Harvard University Press, 2003.

Peterson, Scott, and Peter Ford, "From Iraqi Officers, Three Tales of Shock and Defeat," *The Christian Science Monitor*, April 18, 2003.

Philp, Catherine, "Secrets of Saddam's Family at War," *Timesonline*, June 25, 2003.

Pollack, Kenneth M., *Arabs at War*, Lincoln: University of Nebraska Press, 2002a.

———, *The Threatening Storm: The Case for Invading Iraq*, New York: Random House, 2002b.

Purdum, Todd S., *A Time of Our Choosing*, New York: Henry Holt and Company, 2003.

Ricks, Thomas E., *Fiasco: The American Military Adventure in Iraq*, New York: The Penguin Press, 2006.

Risen, James, "Baghdad Scrambled to Offer Deal to U.S. as War Loomed," *The New York Times*, November 5, 2003.

Sachs, Susan, "A Former Iraqi Officer Denied His Old Post, Fumes at the U.S.," *The New York Times*, November 2, 2003.

Scarborough, Rowan, "U.S. Seeks Surrender of Iraqi Leaders," *The Washington Times*, March 17, 2003

"Security and Foreign Forces, Iraq," *Jane's Defence Weekly*, January 29, 2002. As of February 5, 2003:
http://www4.janes.com/K2/docprint.jsp?K2DocKey=/content1/janesdata/mags/jdw/history

Shadid, Anthony, "For Iraq's Leaders and Loyalists, a Vanishing Act," *The Washington Post*, April 12, 2003b.

———, "Iraqi Officials Emerge, Bolstered by U.S. Setbacks," *The Washington Post*, March 24, 2003a.

Shanker, Thom, "Regime Thought War Unlikely, Iraqis Tell U.S.," *The New York Times*, February 12, 2004.

Shultz, Richard H., Jr., "The Post-Conflict Use of Military Forces: Lessons from Panama, 1989–91," *The Journal of Strategic Studies*, June 1993.

Slocombe, Walter B., "To Build an Army," *The Washington Post*, November 5, 2003.

Smith, Stefan, "Tehran Mocks U.S. Ability to Win Military Action," *The Washington Times*, April 15, 2006.

Solarz, Stephen J., and Paul Wolfowitz, "How to Overthrow Saddam," Letters to the Editor, *Foreign Affairs*, March/April 1999.

Stalinsky, Steven, *Arab and Muslim Jihad Fighters in Iraq*, Washington, D.C.: Middle East Media and Research Institute (MEMRI), Special Report No. 19, July 27, 2003. As of May 4, 2005:
http://www.memri.org/bin/opener.cgi?Page=archives&ID=SR1903

Third Infantry Division (Mechanized), *Operation Iraqi Freedom: After Action Report*, Final Draft, Baghdad, Iraq: Headquarters 3rd Infantry Division (Mechanized), May 12, 2003.

Transcript, "The Invasion of Iraq: An Oral History," *Frontline*, PBS, posted March 9, 2004. As of March 15, 2005:
http://www.pbs.org/wgbh/pages/frontline/shows/invasion/etc/script.html

"Treachery: How Iraq Went to War Against Saddam," *London Sunday Times*, January 11, 2004.

"UK Troops 'Target Ba'ath Militia,'" CNN.com./World. As of June 26, 2007: http://edition.cnn.com/2003/WORLD/meast/03/27/sprj.irq.iraq.basra/

United Nations Security Council Resolution 1441 on Iraq, adopted on December 20, 2002.

U.S. Department of Defense, Washington Headquarters, DoD Personnel and Military Casualty Statistics, "Operation Iraqi Freedom Military Deaths Through April 30, 2003," as of September 2, 2006. As of June 14, 2007: http://siadapp.dmdc.osd.mil/personnel/CASUALTY//castop.htm

Walt, Vivienne, "Chaos Ruled Before Iraq's Military Fell," *Boston Globe*, August 25, 2003. As of June 26, 2007: http://www.hench.net/2003/z082503a.htm

Welsh, May Ying, "U.S. Trains Proxy to Quell Resistance," Aljazeera.Net, June 6, 2004. As of June 10, 2004: http://english.aljazeera.net/NR/excres/554FAF3A-B267-427A-BQEC-54881BDEOA2E.ht

West, Bing, and Major General Ray L. Smith, U.S. Marine Corps (USMC) (Ret.), *The March Up*, New York: Bantam Books, 2003.

Wong, Leonard, Thomas A. Kolditz, Raymond A. Millen, and Terrence M. Potter, *Why They Fight: Combat Motivation in the Iraq War*, Carlisle, Pa.: Strategic Studies Institute, U.S. Army War College, July 2003.

Woods, Kevin M., with Michael R. Pease, Mark E. Stout, Williamson Murray, and James G. Lacey, *Iraqi Perspectives Project: A View of Operation Iraqi Freedom from Saddam's Senior Leadership*, Norfolk, Va.: U.S. Joint Forces Command, Joint Center for Operational Analysis and Lessons Learned, 2006.

Woodward, Bob, *Plan of Attack*, New York: Simon and Schuster, 2004.

Wright, Evan, *Generation Kill*, New York: G. P. Putnam's Sons, 2004.

Zucchino, David, "Iraq's Swift Defeat Blamed on Leaders," *Los Angeles Times*, August 11, 2003.